W9-BLX-390

Between the Eagle & the Dove

Ronald Kirkemo

The Christian & American Foreign Policy

InterVarsity Press
Downers Grove
Illinois 60515

©1976 by Inter-Varsity Christian
Fellowship of the United States of America
All rights reserved. No part
of this book may be reproduced in any
form without written permission
from InterVarsity Press.

InterVarsity Press is the
book publishing division of Inter-Varsity
Christian Fellowship, a student
movement active on campus at hundreds
of universities, colleges and
schools of nursing. For information
about local and regional activities, write
IVCF, 233 Langdon St.,
Madison, WI 53703.

ISBN 0-87784-775-4

Library of Congress Catalog
Card Number: 76-12300

Printed in the United States
of America

261.1
K59

To
Mom and Dad
and
Bill and Frances

56415

CONTENTS

Drawing by D. Fradon: ' 1965 The New Yorker Magazine. Inc.

"Just what do you mean, 'My country, right or wrong'?
Just when has our country ever been wrong?''

INTRODUCTION

This is a book about Christians and American foreign policy. It grows out of my concern over the pervasive distrust of and disrespect for the American government and its foreign activities of the last turbulent decade.

The trauma of that decade was real. The dreadful tragedies and vicious diatribes that accompanied the war in Vietnam wrenched the hearts of sensitive people and broke the bonds of trust between them. The revelations of the Watergate Affair shook their comfortable assumptions about the integrity and truthfulness of the men at all levels of government. These disconcerting and disheartening events have magnified the normal bewilderment people have over foreign affairs. The debate on Anti-Ballistic Missles (ABM), the issues decided at the Strategic Arms Limitation Talks (SALT), the activities of the Central Intelligence Agency (CIA), the kidnapping and murder of diplomats—these are but a few of the many complicated facets of foreign policy that are dimly understood by the general American public even when they know what all the abbreviations stand for.

Christians have been subject to the same attitudes of fear and shock, dismay and defensiveness that have swirled around the country. But it has been harder for them because they had to find how their Christian standards and responsibilities fit with the assertions and activities of the government and the dissidents. Some lost their anchors and were left confused and frustrated in their efforts. Others retreated into a compartmentalization of religion and politics, allowing piety in the church and a morality of the jungle in politics. They never saw the possibilities of ethical action in public affairs. A third group forged a dangerous linkage between their religion and their patriotism, a linkage that enveloped all American politics with the holy glorification of the "Battle Hymn of the Republic." A last group of Christians just stopped caring and became apathetic, weakening the fabric of our democracy at home and the forces of justice and humanity abroad.

But foreign affairs are not easy to understand. The issues of foreign policy are complex, involving ideals and self-interest, humanity and power, justice and deception, cooperation and conflict. What America can do and must do around the globe are sometimes compatible and sometimes not. Leaders and advisers search for right policies, try to simplify and understand the complexity, hope for clarity and adequacy in information, but are still continually faced with ambiguity and uncertainty. Yet they must choose, making decisions in an arena where other nations also have the choice and power to cooperate or obstruct.

Not only is foreign policy complex, it is also passionate and divisive. Foreign policies can animate and agitate emotional beliefs, involve actions that carry immense moral consequences for ourselves and others and suck us into participation through taxation, electoral choice and military service. Policies undertaken with good intentions can turn sour either through the responses of other nations or through some unforeseen weakness in the policy itself. Long-range ideals can be sacrificed to short-term expediency and pragmatism. The desire to help can be corrupted by the arrogance of deciding what is good for others as well as by the exploitation by individuals for their own rewards and personal empires.

The purpose of this book, then, is to help Christians better understand what America is doing abroad and why, and what that implies about the responsibilities and relationships of American Christians to their nation's foreign policy.

This book is intended to be a kind of road map. It identifies major characteristics of international politics, pointing out the contours of relationships and disputes. It raises the ethical implications of various routes to reconciling morality and foreign policy. In this way a person may follow where a particular road will lead before it is taken. Lastly the book presents an overall view of foreign policy. That perspective will aid in relating different aspects and events of foreign policy to each other, putting them into context and thereby reducing dark suspicions and irrelevant debates.

This map unfolds in seven sections or chapters. Chapter one explores the breadth of foreign policy subjects by describing four major world problems causing danger and suffering in the world today. Chapter two describes the essential features of international politics, discloses the central role of power and suggests how peace can be achieved. Chapter three takes up the morality of power and its use. These issues involve how Christian citizens relate to their governments and what kind of moral limits are necessary and possible in the use of force. Chapter four focuses on war issues: the Department of Defense, nuclear weapons, types of war and disarmament. Chapter five deals with the men and institutions that make policy. Chapter six explores the moral qualities of seven possible policies for America and what the characteristics of American foreign policy should be. The final chapter sums up the meaning of all this for Christians and offers ideas and models of what they can and ought to do as they live in this world, subject to two kingdoms, living life between the Eagle (symbol of American might and purpose) and the Dove (symbol of God's Holy Spirit).

In this book I do not presume to tell readers what they ought to believe about the moral nature and ramifications of foreign policy. In that sense it is not a book of authoritarian answers. Rather, I wish to explore foreign policy (an area of great importance and little simplicity) and to suggest relationships between the activities of foreign policy and the standards of Christian faith. But I have not taken space to buttress arguments with catalogs of Scripture. Readers will bring to bear their own knowledge and understanding of the Word, and the Holy Spirit will guide in its application. Each Christian is responsible for determining just what political policies and moral judgments he will support.

I am indebted to many college and Sunday school classes for debating and exploring these issues with me. I want to thank my colleagues for their interest and encouragement, particularly Dwayne Little and Herb Prince who read portions of the manuscript and offered valuable advice. Also, thanks to Reuben Welch and Frank Carver who gave inspiration and counsel from the Word. I especially wish to thank the Alumni Association of Point Loma College for their research award to further the development of this manuscript, though they bear no responsibility for the opinions expressed in it. Special thanks also go to Barbara Thompson for her typing and ever-sharp red pencil that corrected my numerous mistakes.

Finally, I wish to thank Patti, Billy and Johnny for patiently persisting through the seemingly endless hours that I worked and reworked these pages.

I

THE
FOUR
HORSEMEN

"Lord, when did we see thee hungry or thirsty
or a stranger or naked or sick or in prison,
and did not minister to Thee?" Then he will answer
them, "Truly, I say to you, as you did it not
to one of the least of these, you did it not to me."
Matthew 25:44-45

Starving people. Oppressed people. Suffering people. The
world abounds with people like these, people in need.
Jesus has given us criteria for separating the sheep and the
goats in the Last Judgment, criteria that specify the Christian's responsibility to minister to just these kinds of people. Jesus instructs us not to live the Christian life in isolation from the world, not to enter a monastery in callous
indifference to the suffering of those around us. The life of
the Christian involves ministering to the world—sustaining, healing, uplifting and reconciling people.

This perspective is an appropriate starting point for a
discussion of the Christian and American foreign policy.
The American nation cannot escape the world, cannot be
self-contained and isolated. America must relate to the

world. That is foreign policy. How America pursues its own goals and comes to grips with the pressures and needs of the world's problems and dangers is the substance of foreign policy.

Our world is not a joyous, orderly, peaceful place. It is a world with immense problems. And it is a world in which the conditions of life are rapidly deteriorating. In many respects the Four Horsemen described by John in Revelation 6—the Conqueror on the white horse, War on the red horse, Famine on the black horse and Death riding a pale horse—are loosed already. And they leave a trail of sorrow, pain, ruin and death. What should America do?

The Conqueror
The first horseman described by John has a bow and a crown and rides forth to conquer. This horseman is a tyrant. With his bow he extends his power over people through violence and oppression, a Moloch demanding acceptance as ruler. Opposition to his crown is crushed by imprisonment, torture or firing squad. The Conqueror destroys liberty, dignity and truth not only in his country but in others too as he extends his mighty mailed fist.

In Nazi Germany in the 1930s, Hitler led a policy of eliminating the Jews from the face of Europe. In 1972 the small African nation of Burundi systematically murdered a quarter of a million Hutus, an ethnic group in that nation. In South Korea, Brazil and, until recently, in Greece military regimes have grabbed power, closed down parliamentary institutions, banned political groups and discussion, and imprisoned and tortured political opponents into submission. In the Soviet Union opponents are carried off to mental institutions where they are drugged into submission or mental derangement. South Africa and Rhodesia pursue policies of apartheid, fixing in law and enforcing with the Army the arrogant and exploitive domination of a minority race over the rest of the nation.

These kinds of regimes and policies confront the United

States with a major moral issue: Should it be allied with, or even friendly with, dictatorships and tyrants? Or should America use its power and influence to promote democracy and human rights in these kinds of countries?

Believing ourselves to be the kind of nation described by Lincoln in his Gettysburg Address, a nation "conceived in liberty, and dedicated to the proposition that all men are created equal," we immediately shrink from associating with the second-rate colonels and dictators who have messiah complexes.

Unfortunately, a policy of disassociation is not that simple. Two factors must be taken into account. The first was stated succinctly by former President Nixon: "We cannot gear our foreign policy to transformation of other societies. In the nuclear age, our first responsibility must be the prevention of war that could destroy all societies."[1]

The second factor is the limited ability of the United States to force democracy down any country's throat. Contrary to many critics of American foreign policy, the United States has tried repeatedly with different methods to promote democracy around the world. The results have been discouraging.

President Theodore Roosevelt tried to forcibly install democratic governments in various Central American nations in the early 1900s. But when the American military left, either there was a military coup against the American-installed government or the elected leader refused to quit at the end of his term of office.

President Wilson tried to overthrow the dictatorial military regime of General Huerta, who came to power by assassinating the president of Mexico. Diplomatic pressure of various sorts was employed and Wilson at length resorted to the invasion and occupation of the Mexican city of Veracruz in 1914. He succeeded only in generating hatred of Americans among all factions of Mexicans rather than any love of democracy.

General Douglas MacArthur was the Commander of

American Occupation Forces in Japan after World War 2. In that position he wrote a new constitution for Japan and forced them to accept it. That constitution has worked relatively well though the political customs and processes are not exactly what MacArthur intended. But to a large degree the success of that effort resulted from the trauma of total defeat and the repudiation of the militaristic society that led Japan into World War 2. Thus it is not a typical example of a workable method of democratizing a nation.

President Kennedy developed a double-edged policy to promote democracy in Latin America. He announced his intention of breaking diplomatic recognition and relations with any government that came to power through a military coup d'etat and of suspending all economic and military aid to that nation. Additionally, he set up the Social Progress Trust Fund which made very low interest loans to governments for social projects, such as low-cost housing, sewage projects, school construction and literacy programs. But these loans were available only as specific nations requesting them took steps each year to democratize themselves. This approach enjoyed some limited measure of success, but entrenched regimes find it difficult, if not impossible, to reform themselves out of power. The recognition and aid policy did not deter the military from taking power in Ecuador, Argentina, Peru or Guatemala.

These two factors, the primary importance of the war issue and the difficulty of forcing democracy on another nation or expecting it to spring full bloom once a tyrant is removed, lead us to be hesitant about assuming that there is some easy and moral alternative to working with repressive regimes. But, on the other hand, these two factors do not force us to embrace the Conquerors of the world. War is the number one issue of world politics, but there are alternative ways of preserving the peace. And, besides, peace is not really secure in the hands of tyrants who are free and prone to do crazy things with their power, such as the Greek colonel's 1974 effort to topple the government on Cyprus or Burundi's execution of a whole distinctive segment of the population.

America may support the dictators who happen to be friendly because they want to buy U.S. weapons and sports cars. But there may come a time when the dictator is overthrown by a people's revolt. Then America, which should have been on the side of the democratic forces, will be seen as the friend of dictators. Military bases might be closed, corporations might be nationalized and an alliance with an American adversary might be forged.

Finally, if America should eliminate such goals as the spread of justice and democracy to oppressed peoples, an unsought impact might be felt in American domestic society—an unconscious relaxation of commitment to preserve such values for its own people. America might find one day that eliminating the spirit of Lincoln from its foreign policy has gradually eliminated that spirit from its home life.

Then what should be American policy? In between the two extremes of the Exorcist (trying to physically eliminate all repressive governments) and the Puritan (standing back and preaching moral righteousness from a distance) is a moderate policy of undramatic but unmistakable tactics. This allows the United States to be true to its values, its heritage and the oppressed while it works with those whom it must. Such tactics include:

1. In South Africa the United States has placed black Foreign Service Officers in diplomatic assignments as a clear signal to the whites and blacks of that nation that the United States neither approves nor supports the policy of apartheid.

2. The United States could grant American citizenship to political exiles like the Russian writer Alexander Solzhenitsyn.

3. The style of political receptions says a lot. I was at the White House for two such receptions and the difference was obvious. For the visiting President of Mexico,

President Johnson had color guards, military bands and a gracious, cordial speech. But for the reception of the President of Paraguay, a small military dictatorship in Latin America, President Johnson had only one color guard and a very short and cool welcome speech.

4. Democratic "strings" on foreign aid programs can be effective. President Kennedy used his Social Progress Trust Fund program in this way. Nations qualified to receive American foreign aid only if they met certain conditions. Kennedy's conditions required annual progress in implementing democratic reforms in the politics and society of the recipient nation.

5. The United States also funds select groups in a nation, either openly through U.S. trade unions or secretly through the Central Intelligence Agency. America has done this around the world to strengthen democratic groups in resisting the growth of repression and tyranny in their land.

There are many diverse and creative tactics the United States could employ in strengthening forces of justice and making clear its commitment to such goals. But there must be a commitment at the highest levels of the American government to support such goals. Otherwise, while pursuing a balance of power policy, it will be all too easy to slip into a Machiavellian policy of simple power calculation and a moral pragmatism. Many critics of Secretary of State Henry Kissinger charge that this is what has happened. They note his involvement in the CIA operations against Chile, his lack of comment when Solzhenitzyn was under attack in Russia, his silence toward the repressive regime of colonels in Greece and his reprimand of the American Ambassador in Chile for raising the topic about Chilean repression to the leaders of that military regime.

War
The second horseman described by John rode a red horse and had the power to take away peace. This horseman has

ridden this earth throughout its history. War is an ancient enemy of mankind, killing husbands and fathers and sons, destroying homes and livelihoods, distorting economies and inflaming passions. But that ancient horseman has acquired a new weapon—the nuclear bomb.

Why has he had such a free ride throughout history? Why does he come again and again? The particular reasons nations go to war are as varied as men's desires and fears and ambitions. But wars occur because of one factor— there is nothing to stop them. There is no international police force to maintain order among the nations, disarm the violent and imprison the convicted. Nations can go to war because they are free to, and not until that condition is altered will war be abolished and peace reign.

Can that condition be altered, and is support for some sort of international police force an inherently moral policy? There is no doubt that Christians should support efforts designed to protect peace and hinder the outbreak of war. God does not get any particular satisfaction out of seeing humans fight each other with increasingly destructive weapons. He is not a god of war. He does not glory in the hatreds, atrocities and slaughter of humans. Jesus preached love, blessed the peacemakers and rebuked Peter for using the sword against the Roman authorities in Gethsemane. But recognizing the incompatibility of war with Christian principles, one cannot automatically say Christians should support the establishment of an international military force. There are crucial limitations that hinder the development and operation of such a force.

There are three approaches to creating an international peace-keeping force: (1) an international police force, (2) a collective security system and (3) emergency peace forces.

1. *An International Police Force.* The most obvious way to stop war is to create an international police force that will prevent nations from going to war with each other. This force would be stationed around the world and

equipped with the latest advances in military hardware to be able to respond quickly and effectively to an outbreak of violence anywhere.

This force could not be at the disposal of any particular nation, and it could not be autonomous. Either of these arrangements would be too tempting for a would-be world conqueror to use for his own goals. Thus the police force would have to be at the disposal of some sort of international government in which all the nations were represented.

But however desirable such an arrangement may be, the political obstacles to its creation would make it an exercise similar to building the Tower of Babel. The first major problem is the unlikely transfer of loyalty by the international soldiers from their nation to the international government and its force, particularly if the force were ever used against their homeland. Even so great a gentleman as Robert E. Lee gave up his loyalty to the nation and returned to Virginia in 1861 to fight against the Union. What could one expect of less honorable men?

Second, the international police force would also have to be stronger than any combination of nations. It would have to have its own supply of nuclear weapons, and individual nations would have to give up theirs.

Finances are a third problem area. Who would pay for the force? How would the funds be collected from a recalcitrant nation? How could the expenses of the force be apportioned among the nations without having the wealthiest nations demand some kind of political control over the force?

Fourth, the force of world government would need its own industrial base to build and supply weapons. It could not be dependent upon the gifts of the nations or long-term contracts with corporations. One of the main reasons the Revolutionary Army under George Washington was always hungry, cold and in danger was the refusal of the states to honor their supply commitments unless the Army was fighting in their own territory. An international unit, forced to rely on the generosity of nations that were rich and strong enough to make extra military forces available for the force, could be reduced to impotence simply by cutting off supplies.

A fifth problem is secrecy. The force would have to possess its own intelligence unit to provide information on the military capabilities and maneuvers of other nations. It would have to protect its own secrets from officials who would be tempted to pass along information to their home nations.

2. *A Collective Security System*. The second approach is to formalize an agreement among the independent and sovereign nations of the world to act unitedly against an aggressor. They would collectively be responsible for defending the peace by agreeing in advance to come to the aid of a nation under attack. This approach was formalized in the League of Nations and the United Nations. The aim is to eliminate any question that an aggressor might have as to whether or not he could attack another nation and get away with it. Collective security makes it clear to all the world that any aggressor would have to face the active opposition of the whole world.

This would not require a standing international army with all the attendant problems of financing and equipping it in peacetime. Rather, the nations would make their forces available to the United Nations Security Council when requested. The clear, formal agreement of the nations would substitute for a standing army. The control of the police force when put together would be vested in the representative body like the Security Council rather than in some international group set apart from nations.

But collective security in the United Nations was still-born, killed by developments unforeseen by the framers of the U.N. First, the Security Council was paralyzed by the breakdown of cooperation among the Great Powers. Second, wars of insurgency developed, secretly aided and abetted by outside powers, which made the clear identification of an aggressor of an overt attack difficult to determine. And third, the development of intercontinental ballistic missiles armed with nuclear warheads made world war, even when undertaken by the United Nations, too dangerous for the whole world. The U.N. was really designed to prevent another World War 2 not a nuclear World War 3.

Besides these new developments, an old traditional factor renders collective security ineffectual. Nations are not ready to pledge in advance their military machinery and the lives of their citizens to some future war. This is why in 1919 the Senate refused to ratify American membership in the League of Nations. That problem did not exist with the United Nations for the U.S. was the strongest power and could dominate its activities. This situation no longer exists since the nations of Asia, Africa and Latin America now hold a numerical majority in the U.N.'s General Assembly. Collective security, then, is an idea whose time has come and gone.

3. *An Emergency Peace Force.* The third approach to an international peace-keeping force attempts to get around the problems inherent in collective security. An emergency peace force is composed of voluntary military units from neutral or nonaligned nations. No military forces from any of the Great Powers or any of the disputants are included. And rather than being fighting forces, the emergency peace force acts to separate and keep separate the armies of two nations.

Between 1956 and 1957 an emergency force operated in the Sinai Peninsula to keep Israel and Egypt separated while another force operated in Cyprus to separate the Greek and Turk Cypriots. A third emergency force was created in the early 1960s to hold the African nation of the Congo together and to keep both the United States and the Soviet Union out, isolating it from the Cold War. However, it became involved in hostilities as it tried to enforce the union against attempts at secession, a development which cost it the financial and political support of such nations as Russia and France. Another such peace force was created by the regional organization of the Americas, the Organization of American States, and replaced American troops in the Dominican Republic in 1965.

The emergency peace force is able to bring stability to an area by maintaining a separation of forces and keeping out military units from any of the Great Powers. Being a neutral force without Great Power involvement, it is more acceptable to warring nations, and its members will not be partisans subject to conflict of loyalties.

But a major limitation is its inability to bring any reconciliation to hostile nations. Such a peace force only can maintain the absence of fighting; it cannot help resolve the issues. That limitation led to the departure of the Suez force and the outbreak of war in 1967 between Israel and Egypt.

A second major limitation is that such a force can do nothing to prevent the outbreak of a war. It does not really come to grips with the freedom of nations to go to war unhindered. The emergency peace force can be used to preserve a precarious peace only after war has broken out. And because it is not a credible fighting force, it can be overrun or pushed aside as the Turks did to the Cyprus force in 1974.

In summary, there is no permanent way to stop the second horseman. Nations will not voluntarily create an international government that could operate an international police force. And nations are not reliable enough to make a collective security system credible. In the Middle East War of 1973, the India-Pakistan War of 1972 and the Cyprus War of 1974, the Security Council called for a cessation of hostilities. It did not have the political courage to respond by forming an international collective security force. Because of its unwillingness to use collective security measures, its calls for cease fires were disregarded.

Thus, there is presently no formal international arrangement that is effective, permanent and possible which the Christian can support to end wars.

Famine

Famine, the third horseman in John's vision, is not a threat of some future time—it is a present reality. Around the world, but mostly in the Southern Hemisphere, children and adults are dying of starvation and of diseases made lethal by malnutrition.

Some of this famine results from untimely catastrophies like flooding, droughts, hurricanes and earthquakes. But these catastrophies are not the real problem. The famine gripping the world today has deeper and more long-term roots.

One cause of famine is the limited and, in places, decreasing earth space available for cultivation. All the world's lands available for planting are used up. There are no great areas of virgin land that can be cultivated. The dense jungles or rocky mountain slopes that could theoretically be cultivated would require fantastic expenses to prepare. In Africa a six-year drought has dried up water holes, depleted vegetation and parched the ground to such an extent that the Sahara Desert has actually been increasing at the rate of thirty miles a year.

At one time there was great hope for what was called the "Green Revolution," the use of specially developed seeds that would dramatically increase agricultural yield. Norman Borlaug won the 1970 Nobel Peace Prize for his development of these hybrid seeds. But those seeds require much water and fertilizer. Because fertilizer has a petroleum base, the jump in oil prices by the Middle Eastern nations caused the price of fertilizer to escalate. So the hungry nations have been forced to buy less fertilizer. This has two results. First, less fertilizer means less production by a factor of ten. So if a nation buys one million nutrient tons less of fertilizer, its grain production will drop by ten million tons. And second, because one dollar of fertilizer will produce as much food as a nation can import for five dollars, less fertilizer and small harvests mean food must be purchased at a much higher cost from other nations. All of this makes the cost of feeding people enormously more expensive.

That cost in food has been further increased by a significant drop in supplies of food around the world. The United States divested itself of its food stockpiling program in order to save the expense of stockpiling and to decrease supplies and bring a higher price to the American farmer. When the Soviet Union had a bad grain harvest and was going to run short of grain to feed its livestock, the U.S. accepted its cash offer to buy a huge quantity of grain from American farmers, further depleting American supplies. And then the rains came to the Middle West in torrents in 1974, washing out fields and preventing mechanized equipment from working the crops. These rains were followed by an early frost which destroyed much of the corn and soybeans that had survived the earlier weather. By the end of 1974 the world found its food production decreasing and its food costs escalating. When it turned to the United States for help, it found the U.S. in short supply also.

And while food is becoming scarcer, especially for nations that could not readily pay cash for it like Russia, the population of the hungry nations is booming and requiring more food. The figures on population growth are frightening.

It took from the beginning of time until 1825, or all the centuries before Christ and the nineteen centuries since, for the world to reach one billion people. It took only one more century, from 1825 to 1925, to reach two billion. Thirty-five years later, in 1960, the world reached its third billion. And in the next twenty-five years, or by the year 2000, the world will not have increased by just another billion, but will have doubled in population to six billion.

The world's environment could not support or even survive that kind of population pressure.

The world is increasing by two hundred thousand a day. The Far East is adding 37 million each year, even with large family planning programs in both India and China. Mexico, with a population of 48 million in 1970, is adding more people each year than the United States and Canada combined. It will reach 129 million in just thirty years.

In 1798 Thomas Malthus portrayed a grim future for the world. He predicted that population would multiply faster than food production could be increased. The reality of the Malthusian theory has been escaped until now by new developments in hybrid grains, mechanized equipment and vast irrigation projects. But the absence of new lands for cultivation and the increased cost of the new developments are giving new weight to Malthus' prediction.

The combination of population explosion, static food production and world inflation will bankrupt the nations and starve the people. More food will have to be imported at ever higher prices until one by one each nation has no more cash for food purchases and famine begins to spread rapidly. This will create such enormous social tensions that order will break down both within and among nations. Out of the struggle for survival in the underdeveloped countries will come the plummeting of value placed on human life and the rise of dictators and demagogues who will fan the fires of racism and violence.

This deteriorating situation will pose painful dilemmas for American citizens. America faces acute choices because of its large quantities of food and fertilizer. Grains are the basic foodstuffs needed by the nations facing famine, but grains are used by Americans to feed livestock to supply meat. Americans use 1.3 million tons of fertilizer for lawns, golf courses and cemeteries. That same amount would produce enough extra grain in these underdeveloped countries to feed about 65 million people. "If Americans would decrease the meat they eat by 10 percent," noted one authority recently, "it would release enough grain to feed 60 million people."[2]

Yet while American food aid is down forty percent from three years ago, America has given away $25 billion worth of food in the last two decades. America has been generous with the abundance it reaps from its fertile land. Now when that bounty is in short supply at home, the rest of the world needs it more than ever. That raises some very difficult issues and choices for America.

What is America's responsibility to feed these really hungry nations if they do not take steps to halt their booming birthrates, if they continue to take the position that the world food shortage is caused by American imperialism and not population growth? What is America's responsibility to provide food aid to nations which desperately need it but are, at the same time, spending money on the development of military and nuclear programs? Should the United States in effect subsidize their arms program with food or insist that they divert money from those military programs to programs of food production before supplying food?

How should the government choose between cash paying nations like Russia, with its temporary shortages, and the poor nations like Tanzania which need a long-term low-interest credit to buy food from the United States? How much food should the public allow to be exported when it already faces shortages itself, when any further food exports will only increase that shortage and further inflate American food prices? Inflated food prices hurt the poor of America as well as the poor of Bangladesh.

What will happen to the American spirit and conscience if its people, and particularly Christians, watch news reports of starving millions on television during the dinner hour? How callous and indifferent will we become as the crisis mounts?

A World Food Conference was held in Rome in 1974 to find some program of cooperation that would help them stem the tide of famine. Secretary of State Henry Kissinger, attracted by the potential for new developments in American prestige and international cooperation, hoped to make the United States instrumental in establishing a world network of granaries. Like Joseph in ancient Egypt, Kissinger saw how a system of food reserves could prevent starvation in the future.

But Secretary of Agriculture Earl Butz, motivated by domestic considerations, prevailed on the councils of government to reject that proposed policy. Butz led that successful fight against world granaries for the same reason he convinced the government to abolish the granaries it had built up since the New Deal. That reason was to cut down food supplies in order to increase food prices and raise the income for farmers. Because no world granary system would be effective without the participation of American farmlands, the Conference agreed only to set up an organization to monitor how much food was being produced around the world.

The United States could not feed the ever enlarging population of the world even if it tried. Nor can it save the world from famine in the immediate future by technical training and new types of tractors. Inflation has priced miracle wheats and mechanized farming out of the reach of the nations needing them the most. But there are important decisions American leaders could make that would inaugurate policies of service to the needy and less fortunate.

First, the United States should take a place in the vanguard of efforts to promote certain standards of world justice. This would include the belief that all people have the right to a subsistence. No human being, in whatever nation, should starve or be physically deformed from malnutrition while food is wasted in other nations. The right to life should be accepted as a minimum standard of justice around the world.

Second, America's present agricultural policy should

be reversed. A new program of incentives should be introduced to motivate the farmers to produce the food the world needs and still provide them with a fair return on their efforts and investments. For years the American farmer produced too much food. Now that abundance should be encouraged.

Third, some kind of World Food Bank along the lines of the Kissinger proposal ought to be established. That food supply system would stimulate and facilitate efforts by other nations to undertake massive programs of food production. It would divert troublesome suspicions of ulterior political motives in food aid. It would promote adequacy of food supplies. And it would make international and domestic considerations complementary, not contradictory as feared. The food reserve system would purchase all the food the American farmer could produce. Such a World Food Bank would not dictate farm policy to the American farmer. That would be the function of some new farm policy developed by the president and Congress.

Fourth, the United States should insist that the huge cash reserves of the Arab oil nations be used to finance the World Food Bank and to make loans to those countries facing famine. The increased price of oil is partly the cause for world inflation and drop in food production. The bounty from those oil prices ought to be used to subsidize the price of food to bankrupt and famished nations.

Fifth, this world food program could be used as leverage to achieve certain other important goals. Just as President Kennedy's Social Progress Trust Fund had certain "strings" tied to it requiring democratic reforms by the recipient nations, so the United States and the world granary system could require that the nations purchasing food also inaugurate family planning programs to begin slowing the population boom. (That is not a policy of genocide or mass murder of racially different people for the peoples of Asia, Africa and Latin America will always outnumber Americans.) Another requirement could be signature of the

Nuclear Non-Proliferation Treaty so nations would not be spending their money on nuclear weapons and make the world more dangerous.

Terrorists

The Apostle John wrote that Death was the name of the fourth horseman. Death has long been a common feature of the international struggles between peoples, but recently a particular kind of death has been increasingly employed in world politics—terrorism. Terrorism itself is not new; it has long been used by fanatical and psychopathic men against military and political leaders. In fact, it was just such an attack that sparked World War 1.

What is new is the growing attempt to forge a network of cooperation among terrorist groups from different parts of the world. The author of the James Bond novels, Ian Fleming, created a fictional international organization of criminals called SPECTER—Special Executive for Counter-intelligence, Terror, Extortion and Revenge. Such a centralized organization does not now exist, but there is a growing cooperation and mutual involvement by terrorist groups under the umbrella of Al Fatah, a Palestinian guerrilla organization. Al Fatah has run training schools for revolutionaries and terrorists in their desert camps, recruiting young men and women from the Americas, Europe, Africa and Japan.

From those training schools have come a network of liaison and cooperation that has facilitated assassinations and massacres in recent years. In 1970 two persons, one a member of a Nicaraguan guerrilla group, attempted to hijack an Israeli airliner. In 1971 a Turkish guerrilla group, the Dev-Gens, assassinated the Israeli Consul General in Turkey. In that same year four members of the United Red Army of Japan, recruited by an Arab organization and supplied with Czechoslovakian automatic rifles and hand grenades, flew into Israel's Lod Airport and opened fire indiscriminately on deplaning passengers, killing twenty-eight people and wounding scores of others. Later in 1972 the Black September organization invaded the Olympic Games at Munich and kidnapped and later killed eleven members of the Israeli Olympic Team. In 1973 two men carrying Iranian passports were captured with pistols and hand grenades at the Rome Airport. Also in 1973, another Black September gang killed one Belgian and two American diplomats at Khartoum in Sudan. In 1974 members of the Popular Front for the Liberation of Palestine entered the small Israeli town of Ma'alot and killed twenty-one school children. The international aspect of these terrorist operations was further revealed that year when police in France, who had captured one of the leaders of the United Red Army from Japan, had to give him up to Syria when Red Army gunmen invaded the French Embassy in the Netherlands and threatened to kill the diplomats there.

Many revolutionary groups use assassination and terror but limit them to military and political leaders. The distinguishing feature of the events noted above is the involvement of innocent people. Passengers on the numerous hijacked airlines, foreign diplomats and unsuspecting citizens are all jeopardized. At a meeting of revolutionaries in North Korea the chief of the Popular Front for the Liberation of Palestine proclaimed his view that there are no innocent people and, therefore, no political or geographical boundaries and no moral limits on their terrorist operations.

The dangers from these groups of indiscriminate killers are multiplied by their international network of cooperation. Not only weapons and passports, training and information, havens of safety and channels of escape can be provided, but even diplomatic immunity can be obtained from cooperative governments. Thus Daoud Barakat, the head of Black September's Western Europe organization and the man suspected of masterminding the Munich Massacre, holds a diplomatic passport from Yemen and so can travel and communicate in safety as he pleases.

In 1972 the United States introduced a resolution at the United Nations calling for the world's nations to take cooperative action against these terrorists. That resolution was defeated by a vote of 76 to 43, voted down by a coalition of nations led by the Arab states and joined by African states which did not want to imperil any insurgency movements against the regimes in South Africa, Rhodesia and Mozambique.

Two years later the United Nations invited Yassir Arafat, chief of Al Fatah and the Palestine Liberation Organization, to address the General Assembly on issues of the Middle East. Later the Palestine Liberation Organization, a group that represents all the militant Palestinian organizations, was made a non-voting participant at the U.N. These actions by the world body reflect its reorientation from a pro-Israel to a pro-Arab position and cannot but embolden terrorist groups around the world.

International agreements on the prosecution of airline hijackers have been forged and have deterred that criminal activity. But action against these terrorist organizations is more difficult. They enjoy widespread sympathy among the Arab states who control the spigot on the flow of oil. The diversity of their locations complicates efforts to capture them, and the threat that just three or four terrorists can pose to a whole embassy or school or airline makes governments hesitant about moving against them.

But they cannot be given free reign or respectability. If the United Nations will not resist them, then independent governments must. The international police organization, Interpol, can be utilized as can close contact between the national police forces of allied nations. Secret agents can be used to gather information on their operations, to capture leaders and to try to complicate and disrupt their cooperation and operations. Additionally, the United States and its allies can work to cut off havens of safety by exerting diplomatic and economic pressures against nations that grant refuge and safety to terrorists. It is offensive and repulsive that terrorists can commit their wanton crimes and then find refuge in a country. It is also frightening, for it emboldens terrorists by reducing the risks involved for them.

Until Then

Foreign policy cannot be limited to diplomacy and war in a world of the Four Horsemen. The scope of problems that must be dealt with by a nation's foreign policy has broadened to include world social conditions like famine, overpopulation and human rights. Starving people, oppressed people, suffering people—these are subjects of foreign policy just as are territorial rights and military strength. The foreign policy of the United States must be attuned to the needs of people as well as the needs of nations.

It is also clear that foreign policy involves competing issues. The following as well as other pairs of issues present sensitive citizens with difficult choices for foreign policy: (a) human values (the dignity, liberty and equality of people) and the use of violence (war, terrorism); (b) ideal goals (democracy, end to war) and inadequate but possible means (foreign aid, emergency peace forces); (c) domestic considerations (food prices) and world considerations (famine); (d) national policy (war) and individual responsibility (military service); (e) national independence and sovereignty (national farm policy) and international cooperation (World Food Bank); (f) great impersonal forces (famine) and individual personal actions (tyrants, terrorism).

Action must be taken immediately to deal with these problems of famine, war, oppression and terrorism. To delay could well allow the world to slip into disaster, into a New Dark Ages. To delay is senseless. There are alternatives. There are international projects and organizations that can work to alleviate these problems. There are policies and programs available to America which would bring help and relief. There is hope for the world if citizens and nations will work to mitigate the forces of destruction and to build a better world.

This means, at a minimum, that efforts of leaders in and out of the government to stop wars and famine should not be mocked, as Henry Kissinger is often mocked. Henry Kissinger is not the issue. The issue is that such efforts are hard enough without the added burdens and hindrances of such attacks. That is especially true if the ridicule is motivated by partisan political considerations. Surely Christians should not join the chorus of those who snipe at or belittle leaders in government and private relief organizations who are working against the Four Horsemen.

But at this point someone may say, "So what? The Lord is coming back." Yes the Lord is coming back. But people are starving while we wait. People are being tortured and killed while we wait. We can't smugly and piously quote prophecy. That is too abstract, too little concerned with people. Wars kill people and American efforts can prevent some wars from beginning and some wars from worsening. Starvation kills people and American bounty and potential can help alleviate famine.

Even if the rapture is coming soon, we don't drop the Christian lifestyle of love and compassion for our neighbors. The Lord's return should not be awaited with a kind of self-righteous gloating over the increase in wars, terror and famine just because their increase is prophesied. The efforts of Christians to save people from famine and oppression will not prevent or postpone the return of Christ. We must work the works of the Lord until he returns.

We must be concerned with and deal with the tragic present as well as the ultimate future. Christ has made his expectations of us very clear—feed the hungry, heal the sick, support the oppressed and minister to those who suffer due to war and violence. And opportunities abound for such ministry to a suffering and bleeding world through our nation's foreign policy.

II
PRINCES
PEOPLES
& PEACE

*"Blessed are the peacemakers, for they
shall be called sons of God."*
Matthew 5:9

Peace, peace, peace. All the world wants peace. It has been
the struggle of statesmen and the prayer of families since
nations were formed.

Peace? America has been involved in military actions in
all but three years of the past quarter century. Neville
Chamberlain in 1938 proclaimed "peace in our time," but
that peace was smashed by the outbreak of World War 2
just two decades after World War 1.

Peace—how is it established and who are the world's
peacemakers? If we search for answers to those questions,
we will find the essential characteristics of world politics.
Knowledge of those characteristics is a necessary starting
point for understanding American foreign policy and for
developing criteria for evaluating and judging it. We shall

begin by examining two different approaches to peace. One approach, The Prince Approach, emphasizes power and believes that factors such as democracy and justice have no utility or influence in the relations between nations. The other approach, The People's Approach, would substitute the value, the aspirations and the common sense of the world's ordinary people for the use of power, seeing in public opinion a more effective, a more moral and a more natural force in world politics.

The Prince Approach

The name for this first approach is taken from *The Prince*, written by Niccolò Machiavelli to the political rulers and policy-makers of his day. Machiavelli advises,

> A prince should therefore have no other aim or thought, nor take up any other thing for his study, but war and its organization and discipline. . . . In the actions of men, and especially of princes, from which there is no appeal, the end justifies the means. Let a prince therefore aim at conquering and maintaining the state, and the means will always be judged honourable. . . .[1]

This is the Machiavellian perspective: Priority should be given to war; the end justifies the means; might makes right. So the only way to achieve peace is to build a massive military establishment and either smash or frighten all other nations into docile relationships. This design must be followed without regard to considerations of compassion and justice. Ordinary people are selfish and cruel. They too must be suppressed and dominated to prevent the breakdown of society into bloody chaos. The results of this policy will be national greatness as well as peace.

This perspective has found favor in the minds of many rulers who see themselves called by destiny to act as heroes on the world stage. They consider themselves to be above the restraints of common morality. These rulers, or Princes, see themselves as demigods who personally embody the elements necessary for a culture of grandeur whose rule would mold the identity and character of the nation and lay the foundation for a world civilization. They believe their ability and character can be used to seize opportunities and move their nation and the world to greater glory and higher plateaus of civilization.

The people, however, do not possess any grand conceptions of destiny, according to the Machiavellians. The people are too selfish and vacillating to remain committed to goals of grand design. Any setbacks or burdensome costs would immediately cause the people to give up these ends for less ambitious and worthy goals. Therefore the people are to be disregarded. History and world peace are for Princes; obedience is for the people. Princes must move history without regard to the lowly concerns of common persons; otherwise, their grand designs will become weakened, distorted or indefinitely postponed.

One example of this kind of Prince is Napoleon who sought to build an empire engulfing the multitude of territories, city-states and nations on the European continent. Though the empire was built by French troops moving across the continent smashing any resistance, Napoleon sought to bring to his empire the legal system and the values of liberty and equality of the French Revolution. But in the process of building this empire Napoleon took a revolution designed to give power to the people and substituted his emperorship and dynasty. He also took the French people's desire for peace and substituted unlimited wars to the farthest reaches of Europe, achieving not world peace but ever-expanding war.

Hitler is another example of a Machiavellian Prince who sought to forge a new German empire that would bring peace for a thousand years. He unleashed German troops across the face of Europe and North Africa to impose a totalitarian dictatorship on supposedly inferior peoples and justified this effort by asserting the inherent morality of strength.

Both of these rulers experienced failure. Napoleon

wasted the men of his great army and exhausted his nation. When the defeat and destruction of Germany became inevitable, Hitler fought on, intending to destroy the German people for failing to establish his reign of force.

These Machiavellians and their plans fell, as all such rulers and plans have fallen, for their approach to world politics is frightfully wrong. Their self-image as great men of destiny is a delusion to rationalize and romanticize their personal ambitions. Hitler's great plans for his empire were intended not so much to glorify Germany as to glorify himself and assert his pretension to domination.[2] The Prince Approach also suffers from the tendency of the Machiavellian to become so intoxicated with his delusion and power that he disregards all opinions and advice but his own. This restricts his flexibility and warps his understanding and judgment. In addition, a war-oriented rule generates expanded ambitions and so more and more wars. It leads to a conception of people as "vulgar" rabble who must be dominated to end dissent and opposition or as impersonal statistics who are lost in great armies and battlefield reports. It is also a counter-productive approach for it stimulates jealousies and fears in the people and rulers of other nations who realize they must either go to war to stop the Prince or eventually be reduced to submission.

The People's Approach

Visions of an alternative to the Machiavellian approach to foreign policy have abounded. These visions have proclaimed that power is wrong because peace and harmony are natural and normal in life. Wars and tyrants would be banished if the blessed forces of brotherhood and justice could be released to operate unhindered around the world. This is The People's Approach.

President Woodrow Wilson attempted to implement such a vision at the end of World War 1. Wilson's plan had four components. The first was *national self-determina-*

tion. Out of the German, Russian, Austro-Hungarian and Ottoman empires new states were created that conformed to ethnic populations. Wilson believed that empires such as those repress the national longings of people to rule themselves and control their own destinies. These stirrings provoke greater efforts at repression by the imperial rulers, which in turn generates greater hostility and finally civil wars. These struggles prompt rebellion in other empires as well as provide opportunities for other imperial nations to interfere and meddle, increasing the danger of international war. With these empires eliminated Wilson believed these causes for disorder and war would also be eliminated.

The second component of the Wilson plan was *republicanism*. New nations were established with representative governments and the defeated nations were required to abolish their monarchies and set up similar democracies. Monarchies lead to war because kings are free from constitutions and public opinion. Republics (governments with representative institutions) are limited by constitutions and represent ordinary citizens who all hate war because of its costs in money, destruction of homes and deaths of family members. Thus, if all nations were republics, wars caused by unchecked ambitions or daring adventures would be eliminated.

Open diplomacy would, according to Wilson, eliminate a third reason for wars—the existence of numerous, overlapping and threatening secret treaties which commit nations to war without the knowledge and consent of the citizens. The treaties create an interlocking web of obligations that prevent attempts to isolate and contain a developing war, as happened in the outbreak of World War 1. In the place of any future secret treaties, Wilson proposed that all international conferences be open to the public so the citizens of the nations and the world would have a clear view of the alignments and intentions of nations. With this knowledge the people could work through their republican institutions to change any dangerous policies or obligations of their governments.

Finally, a *League of Nations* was erected to represent world public opinion. The League was to have all nations as members and investigate all threats to the peace so that an aggressor could be identified and world opinion could be united in opposition. The League also organized a worldwide system of guarantees against aggression by promising that all members would come to the defense of a nation under attack. With all the nations thus pledged to defend a victim nation, no aggressor could possibly succeed, and so any remaining reason for wars would be checked.

Thus the people would be governed by representative republics. Those republics in turn would constitute a world republican organization, enabling the people of the world to rule their own affairs and to move history on a world scale.

But it was too much to ask that peace would become the inherent and normal feature of the world simply because it was based on a plan that supposedly released the power of public opinion. The peace plan was implemented after the war, and many world statesmen strove to make it work. But it did not work.

The German people and politicians placed Hitler in power. The Italians supported Mussolini's designs of conquest. The Spanish army under General Franco overthrew the republican government of Spain. And when the new nations created at the end of the war were unable to defend themselves and were absorbed by their mighty neighbors, the members of the League took no action to defend them. War broke out at various places in the 1930s and became global in the 1940s despite attempts to prevent it and outlaw it in the 1920s. Wilson's plan to insure permanent peace and to move history by the will of the world's people broke down and disintegrated. The world degenerated into World War 2.

The World and Its Politics

Both of these approaches are deficient. One is too cynical about people and politics, and the other is too optimistic. Might and cunning and grandeur are inescapable pieces of political life, but they are insufficient to build a lasting peace. The public's desire for peace is also real but is too flimsy to support lasting peace. Often it is not as important to them as some other value like protection of territory or honor. Both of these approaches have been partial and simplistic. To understand how peace can be built we need to understand the nature of international politics.

The basic key to such an understanding is the world distribution of power and how that differs from the distribution of power within a nation. England, Burma, Algeria and the United States, whatever their many differences may be, have this in common—overwhelming physical power with the legitimate right to use it vested in the government alone. Enormous varieties of groups and peoples exist in a nation, but they do not have the right to use force to attain any of their goals. With this power the government maintains stability and order throughout the society and provides security to its citizens by protection from physical attack, economic exploitation or social discrimination. It can undertake policies of economic and social change within the nation to achieve greater justice and development and the good life for its citizens. The police enforce both the laws of the government and any court decisions on disputes arising from the law. There is widespread unity among the people on the goals of the government and acceptance of the demands and policies it sets.

But the world outside the nation is quite different. First, there is great diversity—144 nations with different cultures, traditions, ambitions, power, resources; different conceptions of how the world should be organized and the changes that should be sought; and different priorities on the distribution of benefits among the nations. Second, power is decentralized, spread out among those nations.

There is no world government to formulate laws, no world police to carry out laws, no international court to make decisions. Each state has a "free will" to make whatever policy it determines is in its national interest and to choose virtually any means and methods to achieve its policies.

This setting corresponds to the *state of nature* concept employed by political philosophers to describe the condition of men before governments were established. The state of nature is a condition of international anarchy, of total freedom but also vulnerability to the power and will of the strongest. The state of nature is analogous to that condition described in Judges 21:25: "In those days there was no king in Israel; every man did what was right in his own eyes."

Like those of individual citizens, the relations of nations may range from total agreement to total hostility. But nations, unlike citizens, have the legitimate right to use force and violence to protect themselves and settle their disputes. Thus the dangers that exist because of the presence of international hostility are compounded by the open possibility of violence and war. Personal and national ambitions are given full potential in this setting, and history has had a procession of ambitious men and nations—from Alexander the Great to Napoleon and Hitler, as well as the expansionist policies of Bismarck in Germany, Stalin in Russia, and Presidents McKinley and Polk in the United States.

The world setting of freedom and diversity can exist anywhere along a spectrum from complete peace and order to complete war and disorder. International politics can be moderate and peaceful or revolutionary and violent. And in the absence of any international government to maintain peace, the nations must provide for their own protection. They must work in cooperation with each other to preserve international order. In such a setting peace and order are not inherent and automatic. That is a key statement about international politics. Disorder and instability are natural because no automatic harmony of interests exists between the nations, and no international mechanism to prevent war exists because power is decentralized. Thus each nation faces the necessity to give first priority to its own interests and affairs.

The relations of nations depend not only on their ambitions but also on the basic distribution of forces among them, that is, where the powerful nations are located in the world and how they are aligned or divided by treaties. The world powers may be organized and concentrated in two groups or blocs of states, a situation called *bipolar*. This distribution, which occurred in the 1950s and 60s between the so-called Free World and Communist World, increased tension and danger. It eliminated neutrality and forced all choices on issues into only two alternatives, and so amplified confrontation. Within each bloc friendships and cooperation among allies were solidified in the face of a common danger, and the leaders of the blocs developed controls over the other members so small conflicts would not break out among allies. But between the blocs relations were divided and polarized, hostility was unavoidable and though war was less likely because of its extreme danger and worldwide scale, if it had broken out it would have been catastrophic. The international pressures in a bipolar world then lead either to an international showdown and world war or to a search for accommodation among leaders at the expense of principles and escape of the smaller allies from the blocs.

If world power is distributed among four or five great nations, the situation is *multipolar*. There are no long-term alliances among nations and no certain or permanent enemies. A multipolar distribution of forces provides flexibility in policy. A regime can change, modify or reverse commitments and policies with less detrimental impact. It is a less dangerous distribution of forces, too, for the flexibility of commitment and lack of large blocs of states means an outbreak of war will not automatically spread around the globe. On the other hand, that fact makes war less catastrophic and therefore more likely, thus increasing the risk for individual nations who can no longer count on help in an emergency.

The world could also be *imperial*, dominated by one super nation that has reached a position of power far above that of other nations. This world empire could develop either out of the ashes of a future world war or out of an international agreement by nations to surrender their independence to a world state in order to escape the terror of nuclear war. But war would only be eliminated semantically since international wars would be called civil wars. The ability of one group, whether a nation's ruling elite or a cosmopolitan world bureaucracy, to hold together the diversity of the world's population seems impossible.

A final distribution of forces is called *Balkanization*. This is the creation of numerous small nations as existed in Eastern Europe and the Middle East after World War 1. The term implies that the nations are too small to protect themselves from a large, imperialistic nation and too enraptured with their own uniqueness and independence to be peaceful and cooperative neighbors with each other.

The Nations and Their Policies

Three general categories of foreign policies are open to nations: revision, resistance and coexistence.

A policy of *revision* attempts to change the nature of the balance of forces or a nation's relative position in world politics. The purpose motivating this could be one or more of the following.

Revanchism: to regain lost status from an earlier diplomatic or military defeat.

Domination: to achieve new status relative to other nations, such as Iran's policy of building the largest army in the Middle East so it can dominate the politics of that region.

Racism: to reduce or eliminate the international power

and prestige of a state or group of states because of its racial identity, such as the policies of black-ruled African nations against white-ruled African nations, and the Arabs' policies against Israel.

Imperialism: to take over administrative control of distant regions for international prestige, such as Mussolini tried with his military invasion of Ethiopia and as England, France and Germany tried with their economic exploitation of China.

Mission: to create a new pattern of international relations based on a vision of world politics dictated by an ideology, such as communism.

Nations pursuing a policy of revision are on the offensive. They are attacking the pattern of world politics, values and benefits they consider to be unsatisfying, unjust or immoral. These nations are promoting their power and causes to restructure relationships.

Nations that try to prevent and frustrate revisionist policies are pursuing a policy of *resistance*. World Wars 1 and 2 were efforts by nations to resist the purpose of Germany and others to revise the balance of power in Europe and the world at large. The United Nations action in Korea was designed to frustrate what was considered as the inception of a Russian attempt to expand around the world and alter the existing balance of forces. This type of resistance policy is normal for powerful nations which intend to preserve the status quo. It is normal because any basic change in world politics is a threat to their relative position and power as well as to their security. Some of the methods of resistance include the following.

Intervention: to overthrow a government which is thought to be planning or making efforts to alter an existing pattern of world politics.

Containment: to form groups of states by reciprocal guarantees to protect each other against an imperialist power or by acting in harmony against the encroachments of an imperialist in some other part of the world.

Mobilization: to develop or expand economic and military forces to maintain a relative equality in power with an imperial nation. Arms race is the term normally applied to the military aspect of this mobilization.

Satisfaction: to meet, when and if possible, the demands of a revisionist state as a means of satisfying it, rather than forcing confrontation, polarization and enlargement of demands. If the revisionist state is not determined to achieve world dominance, this method can work. If the revisionist state does intend to be a world conqueror, such a tactic is ineffective and may actually be counterproductive by increasing demands. The policy of Neville Chamberlain at Munich is an example.

The third policy of *coexistence* is chosen by a nation if it is unable to bear the strain of prolonged and arduous competition against an ultimately victorious opponent. Finland, for example, is a nation that has the strategic misfortune of bordering Russia, a nation with a history of absorbing unfriendly border states. To prevent such a takeover by Russia, Finland attempts to co-exist by accommodating its foreign policy to the general wishes of Russia. Another kind of coexistence is isolationism, a policy of remaining uninvolved in world politics. America pursued such a policy in its formative years in conformity with George Washington's maxim of avoiding "entangling alliances" with other nations. Both of these methods of coexistence, however, assume the willingness of other nations to respect the independence or isolation of the state. But the fate of Laos in recent years demonstrates that some nations readily violate the independence, neutrality and isolation of a weak state pursuing a policy of coexistence.

But Why That Policy?

If these are the three general alternatives a nation has in foreign policy, what determines which one a nation will choose? The answer is extremely complex at times and simple at others. One factor influencing policy choices is the social values that motivate the general politics of a nation. Politics is the organized process by which a nation attempts to achieve its social values such as order, freedom, general welfare, economic development and so on. Politics are also colored by the social ethics of what is right and wrong, good and bad, just and unjust, inferior and superior. These can influence the goals which a nation will pursue, the means by which they are pursued and the criteria chosen for evaluating other nations and their policies. The social values of freedom and independence of the new African nations, for example, lead them to actively oppose white-dominated regimes in Africa, just as the values of freedom and human dignity influenced the American decision to oppose the totalitarian governments in Nazi Germany and Communist China.

The structure of the government and its individual leaders are other factors that have impact on policy-making.[3] A democratic government with multiple political parties and a representative Congress sharing power with a president will constantly propagate dissenters to the regime's policy. Policy formulation will be infected with the needs and desires of key economic and social groups like maritime unions, defense contractors, Greek-Americans and taxpayers. Policy needs to be acceptable to a majority of representatives. Electioneering requires diplomatic spectacles and policy promises which can lead to false hopes and unwise agreements. Elections can also change leadership and disrupt continuity in policy. To the extent that a dictatorial government has to deal with elections and group pressures, its task is eased by its control of the media and enforcement of secrecy.

Government leaders in America come primarily from the legal and business worlds, and they bring certain habits and attitudes with them. Business leaders, for example, are accustomed to working in groups and making decisions on issues and proposals reduced to simplest terms by staff men. Business goals are limited and specific. "Briefings" replace the need for study. Thus a superficial understanding of issues, a disposition to compromise and accommodate, and a hardening of goals to simplistic slogans are normal. Lawyers, on the other hand, are oriented toward facts about the past and present and so are unaccustomed to planning except to project the present into the future. They are experts at working within a given set of laws to find compromise among clients or to winning technical victories. Both groups then have a tendency to reduce policy to the "crisis management" of issues that were unforeseen, and goals develop a longevity that may far outlast the conditions that originally brought them into being.

Those who rise to power through a dictatorial party reach the top by eliminating opponents and keeping their loyalty to the current "party line" untarnished. They learn to be suspicious, cynical and adept at duplicity, deceit and exploitation of any opportunity or advantage. Nothing in their background prepares them to undertake policies of long-term commitment or to make them effective participants in international discussions based on persuasion or in international conferences based on negotiation and mutual accommodation. Political leaders recruited from a revolutionary party in new unstable nations are predisposed to reckless, adventurous policies in quest of a visionary utopia, in quest of dramatic action to confirm their hero-image and in quest of a supposed enemy that can be used to justify and enforce domestic unity.

Another factor in policy-formulation is the geopolitical situation. There can be great strategic significance to an area like an historic invasion or trade route, the location and usability of a bay, the presence of a channel between seas (the Dardanelles between the Mediterranean and Black Seas) or the potential for a channel (as at Suez and Panama). It is also important whether or not a neighboring nation is a great military power, a member of an imperialistic group of nations or a small, unstable nation that might be occupied by an opponent. Such geopolitical factors can create "eternal goals" for some nations, such as the Russian determination to prevent a future invasion by control of Eastern Europe and to prevent the Black Sea from being dominated by an opponent. But these factors are not necessarily determining. While both England and Japan are island nations in close proximity to a traditionally hostile mainland, England pursued a policy of sea power and world empire and Japan, until the early 1900s, was isolationist.

A final element influencing policy-making is national power. The difference between a desirable policy and a possible policy must always be included in the deliberations and decisions of political leaders. The power of a nation involves such tangible elements as wealth, resources, weapon quantities and its geography. But national power also includes such intangible factors as education and technological level, national morale, government influence over the economy and public opinion, and the capacity for collective endeavors. Like France in 1968, a nation with ambitious designs in the world may find itself humbled by a paralyzing union and student strike over domestic policies. A nation like Finland may desire its own independent foreign policy but simply not have the power to neutralize Russian opposition.

What determines choices on foreign policy? The answer to that varies from nation to nation and varies within each nation over time, circumstances and personnel. For some nations in fortuitous circumstances, there is a constellation of factors that may be weighed and evaluated in motivating choice, giving political leaders great flexibility. Other nations, dependent upon importation of vital resources or occupying a territory that is coveted by other nations, may find options severely restricted.

The implication of the nature of nations and their foreign policies is that prediction of international behavior is difficult and common interests are transitory and hazardous as foundations for national policy. Change is constant, competition and danger are normal and inherent.

Peace, Peace, Peace

What, then, brings peace? How is peace attained and preserved? How can the world be made safe *with* international diversity and safe *for* international diversity?

Peace does not come because nations are friendly and generous with each other since then it would be gone whenever some nation wanted to be unfriendly or covetous and had the power to have its own way. To have peace requires more than just being peaceful and hoping all the other nations will be peaceful too. To have peace the nations must create the conditions that will protect it.

Peace among nations has to be built. Natural peace does not exist. But a constructed one is possible. It results from the conscious fashioning and maintaining of certain international and domestic conditions. Foreign policy, then, must not direct its efforts toward peace itself but toward the creation of balance of power, moderation in policy, legitimacy and acceptance of these by public opinion.

Balance, the first pillar of a constructed peace, is important to prevent any one nation from becoming powerful enough that it can successfully insure (through the use or threat of military and economic power) that its specific demands are met by other nations. Balance comes when nations align and realign themselves in such a way that the sum of their combined power equals or surpasses the power of the threatening nation. In this way its power and demands are either scaled down or neutralized altogether.

This process of maintaining an international balance among nations requires leaders who are adept at manipulating their countries' alignments with each other. They must be flexible, able to shift their relationships when necessary. Such manipulation means that a nation will have no or few permanent friends and enemies. As America has experienced with Germany, Japan, China, Russia, Turkey and others, enmities and friendships do not last forever. The leaders must also be willing and able to work and cooperate with nations they disapprove of, nations whose internal activities are open to criticism but whose support is necessary to prevent a general war. That can be very uncomfortable for nations and their people, but the preservation of peace usually involves neither simplicity nor an easy and permanent division of countries into good and bad.

Lastly, the balancing process may involve conflict, and nations must be willing and able to engage in limited conflict to prevent the balance from being overthrown. If this balance can be preserved, then the ambitions of nations can be resisted. Conflicts that do occur can be kept limited, or they can be isolated and contained within a geographic region before they become global and catastrophic.

The successful operation of an international balance over a long period can lead to the second element of a constructed peace, moderation. Moderation is the absence of grandiose ambitions and intemperate actions, the presence of restraint and toleration. A nation can be induced to be moderate when other nations act together to contain and frustrate its ambitious design, and to accommodate its aspirations whenever reconciliation is both possible and safe. The process of balancing can lead to moderation but it must be coupled with efforts to bring some relative satisfaction to all the nations so that all will find it worthwhile to be moderate. An international balance itself is too fragile, too mechanical. Without the leaven of reconciliation and relative satisfaction, ambitious nations will simply bide their time until they can move and catch the others off guard.

This accommodation and reconciliation comes from negotiations and mutual compromises. We cannot expect the world to be changeless, and we cannot expect nations to be talked out of their historical aspirations and ideological convictions. But if those nations with aspirations and convictions can be balanced and contained, they can be given the choice of no satisfaction of their goals at all or relative satisfaction by mutual compromise. It is then in their interest to moderate their goals. That in turn makes it in the interest of the other nations to be tolerant.

This reconciliation process is not appeasement. The deals and agreements that are worked out must not be based on personal friendships or friendly atmospheres. Rather, the bargains made must be deeply analyzed and thought through to insure that all concerned are protected. This means that the first round of negotiations may not be successful because the goals have not been moderated enough for it to be safe to accommodate. But if the nations can negotiate a mutually beneficial agreement, then the factors of moderation and tolerance will be strengthened and international relationships made more stable.

The two elements of balance and moderation can construct a peace among the nations. But both are fragile and may not survive changes of leadership in key nations or the development of new issues of crucial importance to some. New leaders may not be skillful in handling the balancing process. The advantages of moderation and mutual compromise may not be self-evident to those facing important new issues. What is needed is a concept of cooperation that will transcend immediate problems and justify commitment to an international system of relative equality of nations (balance) and relative satisfaction of needs and goals (moderation). In other words, the nations need a concept of world affairs that will lead them to see a stable world as a legitimate world, a world they feel obliged to protect from disruption. With such a concept of legitimacy, mediocre leaders can be tolerated and new issues resolved without conflict. The great legitimizing principle of the second half of the twentieth century is the commitment to avoid nuclear war. What is needed now is another legitimizing principle to join it, one which would take nations beyond a commitment to avoid nuclear war to a commitment to establish conditions of greater humaneness and justice among the peoples of the world.

The fourth element in a constructed and lasting peace relates to domestic public opinion. The leaders must convey to the people how the legitimacy of world cooperation makes sense in light of their historical heritage and aspirations. They must explain why shifting national alignments and a balance of power are necessary. The importance of participation in world cooperation must be made clear. This is difficult to achieve because the need to compromise is dimly understood by a public that believes its values and policies are right and just. There is also the danger of apathy by citizens who consider shifting alignments to be too intricate or too political (and thus disgusting) to pay close attention. On the other end of the spectrum is the danger that the public will become infected with utopianism and expect far more than its leader can deliver by participation in international cooperation.

If any of these conditions occur, the regime may find its policies emasculated in an unsympathetic Congress. Or it may find itself voted out of office in the next election and replaced by a regime which promises either more "hard-headed realism" and less association with international conferences and disagreeable nations, or more grand and utopian goals. Long-term, patient domestic support is a necessity for the establishment of an international order that provides moderation and stability as well as benefits, all without loss of sovereignty and independence.

The Cold War and the World Today

Let us test this understanding of world politics and the conditions of peace with reference to the Cold War and contemporary world affairs. The Cold War grew out of the particular manner in which World War 2 ended. That global war was fought by the allies to prevent nations of Europe and Asia from being dominated or absorbed by dictatorships in Japan and Germany. Yet at the end of the war the Russian army was occupying nearly all of Eastern Europe, and a communist insurgency movement was near victory in China. Russia, having been invaded by both Napoleon and Hitler through Europe, was determined to make its borders secure with a ring of satellite nations.

The war also ended with the destruction of Europe—the traditional center of world politics—and the rise of two new super nations, the United States and the Soviet Union. These two had been allies in the war. But Russia proclaimed a messianic goal of spreading communism, and America preached democracy and republicanism. Given their disputes over the future of Eastern Europe and their different hopes for the world, they became primary enemies. The stakes of this conflict were raised to new heights of danger when both sides introduced nuclear missiles with intercontinental range. Up until that time nations had to be invaded by armies across borders. A nation could be defended with its own army at the border. But intercontinental missiles made territorial protection of a nation impossible, and nuclear weapons made the destruction of an attack approach obliteration.

The strategic response of America to the Cold War was threefold. The Truman Doctrine was a public announcement that any nation under attack by a communist nation could be assured of American defensive help. With England and France crippled, America took on the role of protecting the world from communism.

The Marshall Plan was a massive foreign aid program designed to rebuild the nations of Europe. This reduced Western Europe's weakness in relation to Russia, provided stronger allies to help the United States defend other parts of the world and solidified relations among the nations of the Free World bloc.

Lastly, U.S. leaders assumed that if Russian attempts to expand around the world could be prevented with a Containment Strategy, then either the domestic pressures against the Russian dictatorship would lead to a new revolution or the Russian regime would finally abandon its imperialistic foreign policy and become a moderate state. In pursuit of this the U.S. created defensive alliances around the periphery of Russia to act as a containment ring stopping expansion. These alliances included NATO in Europe, CENTO in the Middle East, SEATO in Southeast Asia, ANZUS in the South Pacific, and treaties with Nationalist China, Japan and South Korea in the Far East. These alliances created blocs of power that counterbalanced Russia and its blocs of allies. The Korean War signaled that America would undertake active efforts around the world to stop expansion.

Two events occurred in 1956 which had a profound impact on subsequent developments. England, France and Israel attacked Egypt in response to Egypt's nationalization of the Suez Canal. The United States used its authority and influence to force a withdrawal of its allies' forces, raising fears in France that America was trying to run an empire. At the same time a revolution developed in Hungary which Russia extinguished with tanks. That action raised fears in China that all of Russia's allies might be subject to military invasion if their policies did not suit Russian leaders.

In both of these instances the leaders of the two blocs used their power against allies and provoked fears and resentments that would later lead to splits. The next year, for example, two years before General De Gaulle came to power, France decided to build its own nuclear striking force and thereby become independent of the United States. By 1958 Russia began to fear possible ulterior motives in Chinese nuclear plans and so withdrew its nuclear advisers from China. By 1960 the hostility between Russia and China had become deep, bitter and public. This demonstrated that although both call themselves Communist and serve the same ideological prophet, each was an independent nation with its own perspectives and interests. An international bond like ideology or alliance did not destroy the nationalism and independence of nations.

Another major event that began to occur between 1958 and 1960 was decolonization. The European empires in Asia and Africa began to crumble, and new nations emerged that did not want any part of the Cold War. In the United Nations they began to forge a voting majority committed to further decolonization and economic development rather than Cold War issues. To the East-West split between Russia and America was added the North-South split between the developed industrial nations in the Northern Hemisphere and the underdeveloped nations in the Southern Hemisphere.

The early sixties witnessed an acceleration of that trend and two new crises. The 1961 crisis in Berlin led to high tensions between Russia and America and reaffirmed the continued division between the two blocs and the high stakes placed on the territory of Europe. The Cuban Missile Crisis of 1962 led to a direct confrontation between the two Super Powers that raised for the first time the actual possibility of a military clash with disastrous consequences. This realization shook the leaders of the two countries so badly that they began earnest efforts at accommodation that rapidly brought about the end of the Cold War. The very next year both nations instituted the "hot line" between the two capitals and agreed to a Nuclear Test Ban Treaty.

The mid-1960s was an era of confusion as the world began to change. Kennedy and Khrushchev, the two leaders seeking accommodation and relaxation, were both out of the picture by the end of 1964. Their two nations seemed to enter an era of confusion. The fears of being reduced to a satellite in an American empire, coupled with new fears over what secret deals might be made between Russia and America as they searched for accommodation, led France to withdraw from NATO. Fighting erupted between Russian and Chinese troops along their border. A revolution broke out in the Dominican Republic and was aborted by 20,000 American Marines. Ho Chi Minh, struggling since the peace conference of World War 1 to secure the unity of Vietnam and its independence from a succession of empires, sent North Vietnamese troops into South Vietnam. The United States perceived this action as the beginning of a plot by China for a domino-like take-over of Southeast Asia and sent military forces to defend South Vietnam against absorption by North Vietnam.

The Continental Statesman

New policy was finally established under President Nixon and Henry Kissinger, his chief foreign policy adviser. Kissinger, who had studied the great continental statesmen like Metternick, Bismarck, and De Gaulle, aimed to apply their understanding of foreign policy to America's activities. The Russian effort to expand had been moderated and the world of two blocs of cohesive allies had disintegrated into a multipolar world of six major powers—America, Russia, China, Europe, Japan and the Middle East. That new world structure was recognized and accepted, and Nixon worked to gear American policy to a balance of power.

The president re-established cordial relations with mainland China in 1972, a move that jolted some American allies like Japan and added new complications to Russian policy. The next year the president journeyed to Russia and signed an arms control agreement and a declaration of principles. The latter recognizes the common danger of nuclear war and sets forth twelve principles of relations between America and Russia that will act as guides in promoting a legitimate, stable peace. The document specifies the minimum restraints and obligations of the Great Powers. The journeys represent flexibility in alignments among the nations. In 1974, similarly, the United States worked out a new arms control agreement with Russia and warned China three times that Russia appeared to be preparing a land invasion of China.

America's worldwide commitments were reduced in 1969 when the president announced the Nixon Doctrine. This warns the world's small nations that they can no longer count on the automatic use of American troops and unilateral American aid to defend them—in effect a retrenchment of the Truman Doctrine. America will still play a purposeful and active global role but will do it with more discrimination. Priorities among geographic regions and conflicts replaced a policy of full involvement everywhere.

Coupled with the new initiatives to Russia and China was a search for areas of cooperation and agreement. Arms control, through the Strategic Arms Limitation Talks (SALT), was one. But there were many other agreements in medicine, pollution, scientific research, and even a joint manned-space venture in July 1975. Trade was also increased to further link the two nations which once were adversaries.

The policy of detente has many opponents; it is by no means universally admired either in the United States or in Russia. In Russia there is a group of "reactionaries" who fear that Western ideas and aspirations will accompany the trade with America, thereby diluting the purity and zeal of the average communist citizen. Another group of zealots oppose the policy's restraint on Russia's drive for superiority and dominance. A third group, the "dissidents," fears that a relaxation of world tension will permit the Russian government to increase its harsh and repressive rule over the Soviet people.

In America the detente policy has spawned similar groups of opponents. One group sees it as "squashy" or too lenient, too big a gamble on being able to change Russian motivations and actions over a long time period. Another group views it as a fiction, a mask used by Russia to camouflage its real military and ideological buildup. A third group sees detente as a moral outrage, an American acquiescence if not acceptance and approval of the Russian dictatorship. A fourth group sees a stalled policy that is producing far less achievements in halting the arms race than could and should be achieved.

Is detente a cosmetic, masking the true and sinister designs of other nations? If not, and detente is built on an actual modification and moderation of Russian policy, will it survive the deaths of Brezhnev and Mao Tse-tung and be continued by new rulers? Will it even survive elections in America?

There is no sure answer. The diplomat, making foreign policy, is not like Michelangelo carving a timeless work of art from enduring granite. Peace is constructed, to be sure, but not out of stone. Peace is built on relationships which are subject to weakness and change.

The diplomat, when charting his nation's foreign policy, is also not like Galileo mapping the sky and charting the courses of the stars. The trajectory of the stars is immutable. The motivations and future actions of nations are inscrutable. The understanding and predictability of astronomy or physics or chemistry cannot be found in the analysis of international politics.

Those who aspire to truth and certainty in international politics are forced into dogma and become either Princes or Visionaries. Diplomats and statesmen always work at the edge of uncertainty—uncertainty about the appropriateness and time span of policy. Uncertainty is disconcerting, but its alternatives, an American rulership of the world or the emergence of a true brotherhood of man, are "impossible dreams."

The pursuit of detente, then, may be neither correct nor steady in its gains, nor long-lived. Yet uncertainty must not lead to immobility or to a defensive "siege mentality." Statesmanship requires a policy, a conscious and purposeful policy, designed to accentuate and build upon those available positive attributes of today's world and so to move world affairs toward a solidification of conditions of stability and justice.

Questions and Answers

Q. Is there a difference between a Machiavellian Prince and any president or prime minister who shoulders major responsibilities for peace in the world?

A. The line between the two is not clearly and exactly drawn, especially in times of highly emotional debate over a nation's foreign policy. A non-Machiavellian, however, would be distinguished by his willingness to work with other nations in cooperative efforts and to treat other nations with some semblance of equality.

President Nixon has stated that government leaders are on the "great stage of world leadership" and should refrain from the petty, murky, unimportant, vicious things and spend time "building a better world." That statement may be taken either way, as a man obsessed with an historic role and mission or a man determined to use his energy for the benefit of world peace and order. The key to interpreting such a statement is the types of relations which a leader establishes with friends and opponents. Does he seek to dominate or cooperate, to assert himself or to reconcile differences and hostilities? I think that is the test. The president should not reject his responsibility to use the power of the United States to help protect other nations and build better economic and social conditions within newly emergent nations. But simply undertaking world responsibilities does not make him a Machiavellian.

Q. Doesn't the balance of power system you are advocating actually preserve conditions that create war? Isn't the balance of power an old-fashioned, outmoded and dangerous policy?

A. The balance of power does preserve some of the conditions that create war. It preserves national independence and freedom, shifting alliances and relationships based at least partially on power calculations. But these factors would be absent only under a world empire or international government, which is not necessarily desirable and certainly not attainable in the foreseeable future. The balance of power is a policy in conformity with the reality of international politics, rather than a policy based on a proclaimed assertion that a brotherhood of man exists or that peace and harmony are natural and normal.

Additionally, the balance of power policy does not preclude international agreements on weapon regulation, regional organizations to resolve conflict, cooperation in economic and social development, joint space exploration, illegal drug traffic suppression, environmental protection or conservation of the living resources of the sea. So I am advocating a balance of power policy that, in moderating national ambitions, makes international cooperation possible.

Q. But if peace requires a balance, and a balance may require conflict to maintain it, aren't you arguing that peace depends on war? That doesn't make sense!

A. Peace exists when nations do not go to war, when there is restraint from seeking goals by violent means. However, if a nation cannot or will not restrain itself, it may have to be restrained by other nations. Now that amounts to violating the peace in the name of peace. On the face of it that sounds illogical and many critics of this approach delight in pointing out this seeming inconsistency. But the approach I am arguing, while it is unfortunate and tragic, is not illogical or unnecessary. A nation may develop mighty ambitions and become a threat to the international balance in general and specific nations in particular. In such a case the integrity of balance and safety may require that the ambitious nation be resisted.

Q. If peace requires such a power-oriented policy, how can one work for conditions of humaneness and justice among the world's people?

A. In a world like ours, divided, fully armed and overshadowed by the danger of a catastrophic nuclear war, the first concern must be the prevention of such a war. To do that, instability and unpredictability must be reduced by achieving a strategic balance. Mutual tensions and suspicions must also be reduced and defused through mutual and strategically safe accommodations. Once a minimum level of order and cooperation are solidified, once preoccupation can be moved from the danger of war to cooperation, then nations, citizens and private organizations can work within that stability to plan activities of benefit to humanity and world community. Order and stability, then, are pre-eminent. They are also of continuing concern since the conditions for peace, once achieved, cannot be ignored and allowed to disintegrate. So concern with power relationships will retain high priority, but they do not have to be the sole priority once stability is attained.

Foreign policy has a logic and rationality of its own. American leaders must pursue a policy that operates within that logic in order to protect the nation and solidify the conditions for peace. And that creates the dilemma for the Christian, for a policy of humanity and justice and peace cannot be pursued apart from the necessities of political action.

Q. You listed numerous opponents to detente. What, in fact, has detente accomplished?

A. Besides the concrete gains already mentioned, there have also been intangible, but nevertheless real, accomplishments in ridding ourselves of distortions in our images and understanding of each other. That may seem unimportant, but it can be critical in the midst of a world crisis. Finally, deadly events have been avoided. There have been no Berlin crises, no new nuclear arms races and no direct U.S.-U.S.S.R. confrontations.

Now that doesn't mean the Russians are out to help us build a greater American society. With the nuclear arms race halted, there is a new naval arms race. Increased trade has made the Russian communist economy more viable. Further progress in detente is not automatic; it can be halted and even reversed. Detente is delicate, but there has been a dramatic change in the climate of relations as both nations have sought to move away from the dangers of nuclear war to closer cooperation with one another.

The paradox is that as detente works and the horrendous danger of nuclear war is lessened, detente will be taken as natural. If that is done and the reasons or foundations for detente's success are forgotten, many people will call for new stringent concessions rather than mutual compromises from the Russians. That will lead to strained relations. In other words, the very success of detente could set loose the forces that could kill it.

Q. Some nations are inherently aggressive, such as the Communists who strive for world conquest. How can we cooperate with them?

A. The ideology of a regime certainly can have an impact on the nation's foreign policy, but ideology is not necessarily the major or decisive factor. Ideologies can affect attitudes about cooperation, provide a criterion for judgment and evaluation, and establish a vision of a desirable state of world affairs.

But there remains the difference between what a nation wants and what it can get. There is also the factor of public support. If significant domestic sacrifices are required for policies that are continually met with frustration around the globe, then domestic unrest on a wide scale could call the regime into question. To prevent a domestic upheaval the regime will have to temporarily moderate its foreign policy and satisfy domestic needs, waiting for more favorable international conditions. But if other nations continue to successfully frustrate its expansion, then its temporary moderation will become long-term.

Nationalism and national interest have also proven stronger than international ideology. Nationalism—the feeling of national unity and the ascribing of supreme value to the nation by the citizens—has made states reluctant to voluntarily submit their identities and policies to another nation for the sake of an international ideology. The split between Russia and China in the early 1960s was inevitable. China's hundreds and hundreds of years of history and glory made it more desirable to reinterpret Lenin's ideology and become a new prophet than to preserve the world communism's unity at the price of second-class membership.

The national security interests of a nation may be a more persuasive and compelling explanation of state policy than ideology. Russia, for example, would and did desire control over Eastern Europe, the historic European invasion route to Moscow, regardless of the character of the regime. The Russian presence in Hungary is not so much a reflection of communist doctrine as it is of Russian history and geopolitical threat.

Q. But aren't communist leaders irrational, dedicated to world conquest with no concern for the cost, willing to sacrifice their hordes of people for victory over the United States?

A. That was a commonly held assertion, but it does not hold up in view of the actual history of communist nations. China has not been a warmonger nation, nor has it used its nuclear weapons against any other nation. It has, in fact, pursued a very cautious policy, not willing to risk its existence or achievements. The areas that it has absorbed, like Tibet and Mongolia, were historic portions of China that even Chiang Kai-shek stated he intended to annex someday.

Basic Reading

Aron, Raymond. *Peace and War*. New York: Frederick A. Praeger. 1967. A large book of unusual breadth. Aron's approach and insights are extraordinarily good.

Carr, Edward Hallett. *The Twenty Years' Crisis, 1919-1939*. New York: Harper Torchbooks. 1939. A classic critique of the utopian, or what I called the People's Approach, to international politics. Carr also treats the roles of power, morality and law.

Hoffmann, Stanley. *The State of War*. New York: Frederick A. Praeger. 1965. Hoffmann is probably the best writer today in America on international politics. This book is a collection of his essays.

Waltz, Kenneth. *Man, the State and War*. New Jersey: Columbia University Press. 1954.

III
RENDERING
UNTO CAESAR
& UNTO GOD

*"Then render to Caesar the things that are Caesar's,
and to God the things that are God's."*
Luke 20:25

We saw that power is an essential ingredient in world politics. It cannot be escaped. So we must now turn to the moral quality of the use of power and to the relation of the Christian to government and military power.

"Then render to Caesar the things that are Caesar's, and to God the things that are God's." With these words Jesus answered the loaded question put to him by his enemies, escaping their obvious attempt to trap him into an assertion they could claim made him politically subversive or religiously shallow. He gave no encouragement to zealots wanting to overthrow Caesar, the foreign dictator ruling over the "promised land," and yet at the same time he did not submerge the loyalty and responsibilities of the Christian to the demands of Caesar.

The answer silenced his enemies in that day. But what does it say to evangelicals today, to us who have given all of ourselves to Christ in full consecration? What does it say to us in an age when nuclear weapons and intercontinental missiles make the stakes and issues of national security awesome, when media techniques can create crises illusions and mobilize public opinion behind certain policies, and when post-Vietnam America is struggling to find unity again on goals of foreign policy?

The Christian as American Citizen

When a person accepts Christ's call, he becomes a citizen of the kingdom of God. But he does not cease being a citizen of his own country, and his government does not automatically become demonic and evil. A dual citizenship faces the Christian.

The Apostle Paul in Romans 13 and the Apostle Peter in his first epistle call on Christians to submit to their government and its magistrates for government authority has been instituted by God to promote goodness and justice and to punish criminals. That call of the apostles is clear and undeniable. But it is not absolute. They make the explicit point that the government is acting on behalf of right and against wrong and evil. Their call for obedience is the normal principle upon which Christians relate to their governments, but it is not the only relevant principle. Both apostles assume Christians must abstain from evil conduct. Thus, the same theme runs through writings of the apostles as ran through the words of Jesus—there is a realm of Caesar and a realm of God. So Caesar and his demands cannot be absolute if they run counter to the demands of God.

What we need to know is whether the possibility exists for these two citizenships to come into conflict. Can a Christian find himself torn between conflicting demands for obedience from the state and from God, from the Eagle and from the Dove? Can a situation arise in which the demands of one citizenship must be rejected in order to comply with the demands of the other? If that potential for a conflict of loyalties exists, how can a Christian recognize it and what should be the response when it does?

One fundamental issue in these questions is whether or not one's own government can be immoral or act immorally. Every Christian must face that issue, determining for himself whether or not he really believes it is possible for his nation not to be just stupid or wrong or inefficient—but evil.

At this point I want to make some distinctions in terms. There is a difference between the nation, the government and the regime. The *nation* embodies the culture, heritage, people and ideals of a particular land. The nation is constant, permanent in time unless changed by revolution or conquest. The *government* is the legal structure, the offices and institutions, the powers and restrictions set up by the constitution. The government in this country has been permanent since 1789, a unique achievement compared to the histories of other modern countries. The *regime* is the particular administration voted into *government* offices—the president, his appointed officers, his congressional supporters and his policies.

These distinctions imply different levels of obligation and commitment for the citizen. The nation is normally the subject of deep and permanent attachments. This attachment, called patriotism, arises from a complex set of factors and motives that are all inescapable though held in varying degrees by different people.

The nation is a major part of a person's self-concept; it is a homeland that acts as a reference group from which one establishes identity, attitudes, values and criteria for evaluation of issues. When this is applied to a world of separate nations, the result is a division of mankind into *we* and *they*, a factor that promotes distrust, arrogance and rigidity toward other nations. At the same time, this identification with the nation orients one's life toward the achievement of ideals like growth and improvement, community and justice, and self-sacrifice for the sake of others. Identity with a nation also acts as a source of personal security. A citizen "belongs" to a group which accepts him and which is virtually permanent and indestructible, acting as an anchor in the individual's life of rapid and sometimes incomprehensible and hostile change.

Beyond these psychological factors are sociological ones. The style and environment of a person's early years can create certain predispositions and assumptions about politics. A lack of love, an authoritarian homelife or a low level of educational and cultural exposure tends to produce a simplistic, black-and-white view of the world and its problems, a rigid self-righteousness and a readiness to believe demonological and conspiratorial interpretations of world events. On the other hand, intense patriotism can come easily to persons who have found high levels of status, power and remuneration in government or government subsidized careers, like scientific research and aircraft construction.

Finally, there is a social morality created from early childhood in the public schools. History textbooks introduce children to heroes and to appreciation of the sacrifices of early founders and soldiers of the nation. The pledge of allegiance to the flag and the republic for which it stands reinforces this automatic appreciation and pride. The teaching of the English language and other subjects also lend support to the assumed pre-eminence of one's own nation and its ideals and way of life.

Commitment to the government, as distinct from the nation, is supported by two major pillars. One pillar is the government's role in maintaining peace and order in society, in preventing violence and insecurity. Government action to impose restraint and orderly behavior on large groups of people is an indispensable requirement for fallen man who combines in his character, according to the authors of the U.S. Constitution, such attributes as avarice, passion, vindictiveness and sadism. This was certainly the opinion of Paul and Peter when they exhorted early Christians to obey the government for it was designed by God to be a terror to the wicked.

But recognizing the necessity of government in a fallen world does not necessarily mean that all governments are invested with a divine nature. Governmental use of force may be ordained by God to preserve order, but that does not mean all governments are God's governments.

This has been the position of a large portion of Protestantism since the days of the Reformation. Luther and the Roman Catholic Church looked upon specific governments as God's tools in the world; this made them divine organizations not to be opposed. Calvin believed governments are not necessarily Christian but can be made so and instituted a theocracy in Switzerland as the Mormons did in Utah.

Other portions of Protestantism, however, rejected the attribution of a divine nature to government and held that governments are free social associations which must be subjected to the will of the people as well as the will of God. Additionally, these Protestants held that the church should be clearly and permanently separated from the state, for religion is a purely private matter which should not be dictated, distorted or repressed by a state. This position escapes the dilemmas of regarding every government, including those of Communist China and Nazi Germany, as being specifically established and maintained by God. In other words, governments are the means by which God intends peace to be maintained and life made tolerable for men, but that does not mean God is to be blamed either for the types of government created by some fanatical men like Stalin or for the purposes established by some evil men like Hitler.

A second pillar supporting commitment and obedience to a government is, in the case of the United States, its mechanistic, utilitarian and moderate characteristics. The

American government is based on the "social contract" theories of 18th-century political philosophers. They believed governments are created by men for the purpose of achieving certain objectives. Governments are no more than legal machines which men build and use for their common ends. The Preamble of the American Constitution states:

> We the people of the United States, in order to form a more perfect union, establish justice, insure domestic tranquility, provide for the common defense, promote the general welfare, and secure the blessings of liberty to ourselves and our posterity, do ordain and establish this Constitution for the United States of America.

This Constitution assumes the people are sovereign and the government is their legal vehicle for fulfilling six goals that are specifically identified. In short, one owes obedience to this government because it is specifically designed to be utilitarian and work for the benefit of its citizens.

The American government also insures moderation and prevents tyranny, a fundamental objective of the Founding Fathers according to James Madison. This is achieved by creating a split between a national government and fifty state governments which hold independent power, an arrangement we call federalism. Each of these governments are separated into legislative, executive and judicial branches, being further complicated by dividing the legislatures into two houses—Senate and House of Representatives. Finally, the separation of powers is reinforced by the election of office holders from different constituencies and for different terms of service: presidents from the nation for four years, senators from states for six years, congressmen from districts for two years and Supreme Court justices from the nation's legal elite for life terms.

This splintering of the government was designed to prevent any one person or group from gaining control of the government and using it to oppress or exploit other groups of citizens. It is just too hard for any combination of men to capture all three branches and impossible to capture control of both the national and state levels. This splintering also has the positive effect of facilitating widespread representation of citizens in the government.

We can say, in general, there is little likelihood that the commitment and obligations of a Christian to the American nation and government will become an issue for him. But commitment and obligation to the regime—the administration and its policies—are different. The whole arrangement of the American electoral system with its political parties, secret ballots and opposing candidates implies that opposition to persons and policies of the current regime is legitimate and acceptable. Opposition recruits men to public office, hinders the development of corruption in government, prevents a ruling administration from confusing itself with the government and assuming prerogatives beyond the confines of the law, and maintains governmental responsiveness to the electorate.

But how does this opposition fit in with the exhortations of Paul and Peter? It doesn't fit because such legitimate opposition was not contemplated by the apostles, there being no difference in their day between the government and the regime. Pilate, Herod and Nero all represented a government, not a political party. So opposition to them was the same as opposition to the government. It was not until the eighteenth century that monarchies and belief in divine right of kings were replaced with republics and belief in citizen participation and electoral choice, a change that created the distinction between government and regime.

In 1776 Thomas Jefferson justified the American Revolution in the Declaration of Independence by arguing that whenever a government becomes destructive to the inalienable rights of man granted them by their Creator, "it is the right of the people to alter or abolish it, and to institute new government." But in 1789 the U.S. Constitution was written and a new political process was created. With the

electoral structure established by the Constitution, undesirable or unjust policies could be changed without overthrowing the government. The government would remain
permanent while various regimes and policies would be
voted in or out of power.

Law and Obedience

Disagreement with the policies and leaders of a regime and
electoral opposition and voting against them are within
the boundaries of morality. But is it still moral when that
opposition involves actions which violate the law? Should
a Christian break the law in opposition to an immoral
regime?

In seeking an answer to that question we must recognize
the immense importance of law and order in society. Moderation, trust, predictability and security are dependent
upon order. Lawlessness or widespread disregard for the
law or the use of extremist tactics destroy the conditions
for social growth and justice. In such a situation, as Shakespeare pointedly wrote,

Force should be right; or, rather, right and wrong...
should lose their names, and so should justice too.[1]
Additionally, attitudes and habits of disrespect for the law
can spread to large segments of the population. And numerous countries have seen lawlessness used as a rationale for the imposition of authoritarian policies or for the
takeover of the government by the military, an organization with the power to enforce peace. For, as Thomas
Hobbes put it, "When nothing else turns up, clubs are
trumps."

Yet these dangers of lawlessness are not the whole picture. Law is not a neutral, objective tool of society operating equally for the good of all. The functions of regulation,
authorization and suppression in law are used to achieve
certain ends. Law is purposive. Law can be used to benefit
one group at the expense of another, whether these groups
are identified by wealth (or the lack of it), color, national

origin or political goals. Law can be used to abolish one set of conditions (like slavery, child labor or unemployment) and establish another (like integration, woman suffrage or energy rationing). Law can be used to allow one type of action (such as freedom of worship or publication of pornography) and prevent another (such as prayer in schools or compulsory unionization).

This issue of whether or not a Christian should break the law is seen in its starkest terms in the Germany of the 1930s. Law was used to confiscate the wealth and property of one group of persons—the Jews. Legal control of the media was used to create attitudes and behavior of social discrimination against them. Then the law was used to authorize and carry out their mass murder. What should have been the Christian's duty to that regime and its laws? Could a Christian have run the concentration camps that held those pecple like animals until their time of execution? Could a Christian have opened the gas chambers and furnaces that destroyed six million people? Even if not so directly involved, should the Christian have supported Hitler's drive into Poland, France, Russia, Belgium, Rumania, Finland, Norway, Denmark, Egypt, Algeria and Lybia? And should the Christian have submitted to the government demand to be a part of the imposition in those conquered territories of a master race built on the glorification of violence and the reduction of the inhabitants to conditions of slavery? If the answer is no, as it must be, the reason is the existence of values and principles of greater importance to the Christian than loyalty to a law and desire for social order.

Law is a tool of a regime, a secular tool of a secular kingdom. Laws are not inherently ordained by God. The secular nature of law does not automatically release Christians from obligations of obedience to it because an attitude of lawlessness could develop that would destroy peace and order.

But specific laws can be quite unjust, quite immoral. In

the twentieth century the world has seen Russia and Germany come under the control of groups that turned those nations into near replicas of the Beast prophesied in Revelation 13. As for Christians in those countries, Christ did not immediately return and the government did not immediately fall. Laws and regimes can be unjust and demonic. There is no assurance that one would have to obey them for only a short time until Christ returns or until the regime is abolished. Therefore the Christian cannot hold the view that obedience to all laws is a permanent requirement in all circumstances.

But can a person oppose a regime and its policies by not following unjust laws and still not be opposing the government? That question was answered for Americans in the early years of their country's history. The Federalist administration of President John Adams strove to maintain the principle that the administration and the government were identical. As the election of 1800 approached the Alien and Sedition Acts were passed to prohibit criticism by the newspapers and stop the rise of opposition political parties. Those obviously tyrannical laws were not complied with in the election campaign, and Jefferson allowed them to expire when he became president the next year. It is possible to oppose and resist a regime and its policies without resisting and opposing the government and all political authority.

Yet that distinction does not occur automatically. It is hard to make and maintain when accusations and countercharges become emotional and polemical. A person choosing such opposition must make very clear the specific nature of his opposition. If he does not, he will be labeled a subversive, and his actions and influence could contribute to a general breakdown in respect for the rule of law.

It was tremendously difficult in the late 1960s for persons actively opposed to the Vietnam War but not to the government or American society in general to differentiate themselves from the general anti-American tone of the hippie/yippie groups. Part of the reason was the media's fascination with the more militant and dramatic groups, and part of the reason was the political tactic of asserting that all the opponents of the war fit into a single category of extremists.

If it is possible to oppose a regime, why did Christ not authorize Jewish opposition to the alien Roman imperial government? It may be that the Roman government, while foreign and imperial, was not particularly evil for its time, and Christ had no particular reason under those conditions to do anything that would divert attention from his message. He did reaffirm the legitimacy of government, but he did not bind his followers to perpetual obedience in the verse quoted at the start of this chapter. He made clear that certain areas of Christian life were to be rendered to God and not to Caesar. Caesar has his due, but his sphere is limited.

One final question should be noted. If elections are held every four years under the American Constitution, why be concerned about breaking the law? Why not just wait until the next election and try to elect a different regime? First, four years is a very long time to allow the unrestrained propagation of an immoral policy. Great destruction, both physically and emotionally, can occur in that time. Secondly, there is no assurance that a regime pursuing an immoral policy will allow freely contested elections, and there is no assurance that a majority of voting citizens will share the view that a particular policy is immoral. The voting public is not a Christian public entirely.

In summary, government power is not inherently evil or divine. It is a fact of social life, a tool that can be employed for evil or good purposes. It is incumbent upon Christians, then, to be ever watchful of the purposes, the methods and the consequences of government power. It is a duty of Christians to support government authority when it pursues justice and order in society. But support or opposition to particular regimes and policies is natural in a democratic republic.

But what about the use of government power outside the nation's borders? Is it inherently moral or immoral to use government power against other nations and their peoples? particularly war and the threat of force and destruction? There are four general categories of how morality and foreign policy can be related: the Eagle Glorified (or the Crusade), the Pacifist, the Realist and the Just War.

The Eagle Glorified

As a ruling institution the government has authority over other groups and organizations in society, placing it above individual means. When the features of authority and elevated prestige are combined with the historical continuity and permanence of the nation, the state can take on the appearance of a transcendent entity. And that quality can make it seem like a moral being. It can become a transcendent, moral master whose prestige and welfare are the standards for judging actions and attitudes, and whose goals of fame and power provide purpose and meaning. The state is transformed into a glorified semidivinity that receives a patriotism so intense that it borders on religious fervor and that provides a mantle of morality which envelops those who praise it, support it and carry out its policies. Some Christians who have held this view have unnecessarily interlocked their obligation to Christ and their obligation to this moral state.

Another similar perspective belongs to those who believe God has divinely ordained and blessed their nation. Possible reasons for this are that its people and government are far superior to those of other nations, that the Founding Fathers (despite their deistic beliefs) are idealized as agents of God assigned to the task of creating a "Christian nation" or that all governments are God's tools and are therefore holy and blessed. Whatever the reason those in this category believe they have a moral and even religious duty to carry out the policies of their nation.

Major James M. Hutchens, a chaplain to the Green Berets—the U.S. Special Forces or guerrilla forces in Vietnam —wrote a book concerning his experiences in Vietnam. He included this perspective:

"Chaplain," some asked, "why are we going to Vietnam?" To these I read the Word of God in chapter 13 of the epistle to the Romans: "Let every soul be subject unto the higher powers. For there is no power but of God; the powers that be are ordained of God." In this subjection to a properly constituted governmental authority the soldier finds himself serving as the arm of God that bears the sword. This sword brings retribution upon those who defy an institution authorized by God.[2]

If this perspective takes root in the mind of the individual, it is easy to jump as Hutchens does to a religious glorification of the soldier and martial virtues. Discipline, bravery, valor, strength, high sense of duty, strong defense of one's prerogatives, a commanding self-confidence—these become religious qualities in a highly romanticized military setting.

For example, at Valley Forge in Pennsylvania, the site of the winter quarters of George Washington and his troops during the Revolution, a chapel with beautiful stained-glass windows has been built. But portrayed on those stained-glass windows in that Christian building are not Christian saints but Revolutionary War heroes. Another example is the chapel of the Virginia Military Institute in Lexington, Virginia. Behind the altar in that chapel hangs a huge painting of an infantry charge during the battle of the Civil War.

President Theodore Roosevelt proclaimed that citizens who did not possess these martial qualities, who substituted their own personal ease for high ideals and sacrificial service to the nation, would soon lose their own sense of morality and capacity for moral action. Additionally, their refusal to immediately defend their own rights and self-defined prerogatives would actually promote evil by encouraging the wrongdoer. A nation must also have these same qualities, Roosevelt argued, for international politics is a world of Social Darwinism where only the strongest nations survive, a survival-of-the-fittest world where nations must be constantly ready and willing to use every opportunity to increase their power and prestige. National self-centeredness and assertiveness is morally right since in the context of world politics it promotes ideals, hinders evil, protects rights and promotes the martial virtues among its citizens. The martial spirit is emphasized because it is seen as the method for coping with man's destructive forces. The soldier symbolizes self-control, resistance to evil and inspiration for mastery of the physical and spiritual potentials in life.

One of the key features of this approach, the interlocking of Christian obligation to God and to the state, is not a necessary connection. Christ taught limited obligation to the state and certainly rejected any indication that it was an organization that warranted this kind of adoration.

There is a second problem in Hutchens's argument. If governments are ordained by God, how could a soldier ever fight any government without fighting God and his purposes? If governments are ordained by God, that must include the Russian, North Korean and Chinese as well as the British, French and American. But Hutchens clearly believes the North Vietnamese should have been fought. His escape clause is the phrase "a properly constituted governmental authority." That phrase is not found in the writings of Paul or Peter. It is a political criterion injected by Hutchens. With that phrase he can remove from the protection of Scripture any government that comes to power through a revolution or military coup d'etat as in Russia or China. But if we take the term American Revolution seriously, Hutchens cuts the scriptural ground out from under his own nation. The way to prevent that is to eliminate consistency. Then the Scriptures could be applied or withdrawn on the basis of one's political preferences. But such use of Scripture lacks basic integrity.

This leads to a third problem, the dovetailing of Christian ethics with the particular policy being followed by one's nation. If America fought in Vietnam because North Vietnam was communist, and therefore atheist, why not fight China or Albania? If we fought because North Vietnam was attempting to extend a totalitarian rule to another nation and if we are our brother's keeper, were Americans less than Christian for not fighting with England against Napoleon or for being neutral during the early days of World War 1 or for not trying militarily to stop Russia's occupation of Eastern Europe or for not joining with the Hungarians in 1956 or the Czechoslovakians in 1968 when those nations tried to throw off the domination of Russia? There is a danger that one's perspective of his moral duty will be simply what his government's policy is at any particular time.

We cannot make the attributes of the soldier religious any more than we can the policies of the nation. Personal characteristics like bravery and discipline and valor are good. But if overly glorified, as they were with the Gestapo in Nazi Germany, they can lead to an exceedingly destructive arrogance.

Does this mean the nation is not to be valued and appreciated? Are we to reject the sentiment of Charles De Gaulle when he wrote, "France cannot be France without greatness"? No. The nation and good government are rare and precious commodities. But the motivations for national greatness, the kind of greatness desired and the means to achieve that greatness must all be brought under the judgment and kept within the moral bounds of Christian principles.

Adoration of the nation cannot be compartmentalized and isolated from one's Christian commitments, or it will develop what Machiavelli called a civic religion. Neither can the nation be glorified so that it becomes a false god in itself. Instead, the nation as a secular institution must always be the object of moral scrutiny to insure that it serves and does not supplant ethical goals.

Albert Camus tried to explain to a Nazi friend why the French people reject militarism and violent glory. The approach he enunciated should be similar to that of the Christian.

> We had formed an idea of our country that put her in her proper place, amid other great concepts—friendship, mankind, happiness, our desire for justice. This led us to be severe with her. But in the long run, we were the ones who were right. We didn't bring her any slaves, and we debased nothing for her sake.[3]

The Pacifist

Clearly the concern of Christ's teaching and preaching was not to reaffirm the life of the warrior. He did not come and die so that his followers might be more obedient to the government and more joyful in advancing its policies and claims.

Pacifists reject the crusade ethic of the Eagle Glorified position as a complete misunderstanding of the logic of the Scriptures. They see that Jesus came to bring spiritual liberty by investing the old law with new meaning and power, not reaffirming its bondage. Jesus came to expose the state as a secular, selfish structure, not to glorify it. He came to show a new way of life, not to certify the old life of jealousy, division and conflict. He came to teach purity of heart and action, love of brother and enemy, nonparticipation in evil and nonresistance to persecution. This reading of the Scriptures leads pacifists to reduce their loyalty to the secular, selfish state. And it leads to the view that killing, even in a war, is clearly prohibited to followers of Jesus. Warfare is a harlot a person committed to the way of the Lord cannot be joined with.

Pacifists are united in their opposition to killing even in the name of the nation. The nation and a government invested with police power are necessary in a fallen world, but their functions should not involve the deaths of other people. War is evil. It dehumanizes, mutilates and kills. It promotes hatred, brutality, corruption and atrocities. It does not bring peace; it brings about the sentiments and conditions for a future war.

While there is unity in opposition to war, there is variety among pacifists on the appropriate role for the Christian and on the effect their position will have on society. Some pacifists believe the rejection of war and killing is a personal decision of the Christian that will bring him persecution and have no impact on society at large in the immediate future. These reaffirm the commitment of Daniel's three friends to abstain from evil even if God does not protect them. Persecution may come and evil may spread, but it is enough that their purity has been protected.

Other pacifists believe they should establish a new community either within their nation or outside it. This new community would be based on love and service, and would serve as a witness to the rest of the world that people can live without war and killing, that the belligerence of the soldier is not innate. This kind of pacifism believes that love and service can be a leaven to transform the world. Albert Schweitzer exemplified this when he left his nation and worldly honors to establish a hospital community in Africa. His life was a dramatic rejection of this world's glory and power, and a testimony to a life of love and service.

A third group of pacifists reject this withdrawal approach. They believe war is so evil that a Christian is derelict if it goes unopposed. A Christian should actively campaign against war. Some believe they can be politically effective enough to lay the foundation for the nation's turning away from war as a national policy. Others believe that is too optimistic but that particular wars can be resisted. These pacifists believe that by working to mobilize opinion and pressure groups in the nation they can convince the leaders that the initiation or participation in a particular war will be too costly to these leaders' political futures. In this case the nonviolent processes of government can be used against evil policies. If they are ineffective, if they cannot reverse government policy, then they must resist that policy, resist it actively but nonviolently.

But is it true that the Scriptures teach pacifism? The theology of love and service are certainly clear and unmistakable but not pacifism as a direct derivative. Nor is the tendency to chop off the Old Testament a clear imperative of living under the New Covenant. The basis of pacifism can be found in the Scriptures, but it is not indisputably a necessary element in the Christian life.

There are other evils besides war. And the tendency of some pacifists to accept them in order to protect themselves from the one evil of war seems shortsighted. Killing is not the only means by which people are dehumanized. Tyrants and prophets of new political worlds have commonly debased persons in particular and people in general.

In a moving phrase the author of *Dr. Zhivago* refers to the fate of a young woman in Stalin's Russia as "a nameless number on a list that was afterwards mislaid."[4] Whether it's the Gulag Archipelago, concentration camps in Russia, Auschwitz and the Nuremberg Laws that reduced Jews to slavery and extermination in Nazi Germany or the nameless centers of torture and repression in some contemporary countries, political leaders have and still do dehumanize people for the sake of their political purposes. And when such a nation begins to extend its dominion to one's own people, surely the ethics of love and service do not require Christians to allow that extension in the name of peace.

Is perfect love the absence of killing? Does one have to not kill in order to be holy? In general, yes. And Christians should strive hard to reinforce and support those conditions that reduce the need for killing. But God did not abolish the state or obedience to it. In this world God and Caesar still have recognized realms. And when one Caesar goes "mad" and jeopardizes the societies, the humanity and even the lives of other men, Christians are faced with the requirements of their responsibility to their brothers and sisters. To stand by idly and watch the triumph of that sort of evil seems to be a rejection of all but concern with one's own purity.

A Christian does not have to like wars or support all wars. There are different kinds of wars and different kinds of evil. And to allow the complete triumph of one evil in order to completely refrain from another is not responsible. The pacifist is right in abhorring the killing of war. But the pacifist ethic ought not be applied in an absolute fashion to all times and circumstances.

The Realist
The realists begin with the biblical truth that fallen man is flawed in nature, that inherent in his being are sinful, cruel and selfish characteristics. These lead him to incessant designs for gaining power. Excessive control of one man by another is considered to be unjust. These features of man's nature also mean that all actions and ideals are infected with the virus of egotism and pride, and that all rulers are tempted with the selfish and incompassionate use of their power.

The pride, selfishness and arrogance of the individual are called into judgment by Christian morality for Christ taught love and service. But at the level of national society these realist scholars and theologians recognize that men project their frustration and lack of fulfilled ambitions onto the nation. The state is a corporate personality to which the individual can transfer his repressed longing for power, command and respect. Behavior and attitudes which both he and his society would condemn if carried out by an individual are supported and applauded when carried out by the state. The Christian needs to recognize, therefore, that the state does not just repress evil and anarchy. The state also serves as a vent for individual egoism, pride and will to power, and provides a rationale and legitimacy for the continued harboring of deep attitudes of belligerence, hatred, pride and revenge.

Man's flawed nature motivates policies of expansion and dominion by the nations of the world, policies which other nations must resist for their own protection. Thus the use of force is indispensable. But this raises tensions, dilemmas and paradoxes for the Christian, for the use of force is contrary to the written Word of God. Faced with these dilemmas, the realists call for national policies that will minimize international ambitions, and they call for the acceptance of a dual code of morality.

A nation's foreign policy should accept the reality and necessity for focus on its national interests but also recognize the national interests of other nations. This will allow the achievement of vital interests and also support a determination to check any dangerous ambitions by another nation. It will preserve an international balance of power. Additionally, this recognition of the legitimate national interests of other nations will prevent one's own nation from developing exaggerated moral righteousness or expansive ambitions.

Because this type of competitive, power-oriented behavior is so antithetical to Christian precepts of peace and love, realists call for a dual morality. The nation must operate on the basis of international political reality, and its citizens must support it in international competition. This competition involves the use of power, war, pride and destruction of others. The Christian must recognize the necessity of these types of action and attitudes. The moral code of the individual is not operative for pacifism leads to defeat. Therefore he is forced to support power and politics and rely on the grace of God to understand and forgive. In the words of John C. Bennett,

The gospel, as understood by Christian realism, makes it

possible to choose when all possible choices stab the conscience. . . . The gospel of grace does enable Christians to face the realities of history and to assume their responsibility without paralyzing guilt.[5]

In this context, spiritual principles become subordinate to political principles. Even though the use of power is recognized as evil, how national leaders can use it to pursue the national interest becomes primary.

This, however, does not involve the abandonment of every restraint on the use of force. These writers do exhort political leaders to reject moralism and national righteousness and act with humility toward others. But what would prevent a leader from doing away with restraint? The subordinate morality of the individual? If public opinion accepts the nation's right to claim its goals as moral, and thus hold a self-centered world view, what will prevent the citizens of one country pressing their own goals as inherently superior to those of all other countries? The answer is that nothing can do this except by calling into question the morality of the goals of one's nation.

The realists exhort political leaders to at least try to minimize the intrinsic immorality of their acts when they cannot act morally. They should choose actions that are at least at variance with principles of Christianity. Leaders should not refrain from evil but choose the lesser of two evils.

The realist position was a major new factor in the political debates of the 1930s and 1940s. It received wide distribution through such magazines as *Christianity and Crisis* and *Worldview*. Reinhold Niebuhr's book *Moral Man and Immoral Society* made clear the dangers of moral pretensions by nations and the projected egotism of its citizens. Hans Morgenthau's *Scientific Man Versus Power Politics* and *Politics Among Nations* gave warnings and pleas to political leaders immediately after World War 2 to base future American foreign policy on power politics rather than on idealistic assumptions about the rationality of man and his peaceful intentions. These greatly respected scholars unabashedly pointed out the nature of fallen man and the implications of this on politics.

One of Niebuhr's themes has been a call to deflate the moral smugness and self-righteousness of nations. But despite that warning the realist position nonetheless contains elements that make individual morality vulnerable to national morality. Once the nation becomes the focus of attention, requiring policies and action that "stab the conscience," then personal morality is simply relegated to secondary concern. There is a dual morality, but the two moral codes are not equal—the political code must take precedence, and we are reduced to servants of the state with only great hope in the grace of God.

Additionally, the emphasis on the choice among the lesser of two evils becomes a detour away from policies that can create elements of international community. With primary attention devoted to factors of tangible power and national self-interest, programs of international justice will be seen as wasteful and unnecessary uses of resources. At the same time the constant proclamation on inherent selfishness and pride in all actions reduces the usefulness of constructive policies. Other nations will suspect them, and we ourselves will regard them cynically and believe they are promoted from the unseen advantage of some existent or imagined profiteering elite.

The Just War

The Just War doctrine is held by the Roman Catholic Church and some Protestant theologians such as Paul Ramsey of Princeton Theological Seminary. It asserts that nations are obliged to conform their conduct to Natural Law which permits war for just causes so long as it is conducted within certain moral limits.

In Roman Catholic thought, the state is a divinely ordained institution that is natural to man. The state is not simply the legal machine created by men for their own utilitarian purposes but is created by God for his purposes. The state is not, therefore, an evil seizure of power by the strong over the weak or an amoral legal vehicle.

Moral conduct for the state is not the same as moral conduct for the individual. Power and its use is natural in the environment in which the state acts, and self-defense is a requirement for the protection of citizens, culture and Christian values. Thus a dual morality again exists, but unlike that of the realists, the morality of the state is not in competition or contradictory to the individual's moral responsibilities or principles. The moral code of the state is embodied in Natural Law, a law of nature or the universe that prescribes standards for social and political justice. This Natural Law permits war for states since it is indispensable in their environment, but permits it only under certain conditions.

The first qualification of a Just War is that it cannot be one of aggression, even if motivated by retribution or retaliation. The war must be designed to preserve a condition of justice from destruction or domination by a grossly unjust power. Wars cannot be fought for bad causes.

A second qualifying condition is that the war must be the last resort of the nation. Diplomacy and threat and all other means of resolution must be exhausted. A war, even when it does qualify as a Just War, is still not a good or desirable action, Augustine writes, because of its heavy costs and burdens. Therefore it cannot be entered into lightly. Even a Just War is to be avoided if some other means can be found to be effective.

The third requirement is that the war must be declared by the nation through its constitutional processes. This is not a small technicality. The moral conscience of individuals must have the opportunity to be unified and channeled. If every person could determine for himself the morality or immorality of a war, the state would not be able to act. This requirement gives the benefit of doubt to the state and leaves the burden of proving the immorality of the war to the individual. It is also a method of warning so that the other state involved might cease its offensive actions before actual hostilities begin. Finally, this prohibits clandestine or surprise attacks against unsuspecting nations, thus insuring the defensive nature of the military action.

A final condition for a Just War is the standard of proportionality. The war must have a reasonable chance of success. The war must not be undertaken if it will do more harm and damage than the threat it tries to eliminate. And specific actions in the conduct of the war must not involve more destruction than is necessary to achieve the objective.

The Just War doctrine has some obvious weaknesses of its own. The ability to determine the justness of the cause of the war is exceedingly difficult when one's own nation is involved. Rarely, if ever, does a nation admit that it is fighting for an unjust cause—even Hitler preached the rightness of wars. Additionally, the supposed righteous nature of the state cannot be assumed to make it sensitive and responsible to considerations of justice outside its own self-interest. Because a government is ordained by God in general does not make the regime's policies equivalent to standards of justice.

Evaluating the costs of the war before it starts, and comparing that cost against an evaluation of the threat, is no easy task. The perception of threat, the value placed on the lives and property that will be destroyed, the confidence in the altruism of one's regime and its good faith in finding alternatives to resolving the conflict—these are all factors that are subjectively weighed by individual persons with different values, preferences, fears and heritage. According to Winston Churchill,

> The Statesman who yields to war fever must realize that once the signal is given he is no longer the master of policy but the slave of unforeseeable and uncontrollable events. Antiquated War Offices, weak, incompe-

tent or arrogant Commanders, untrustworthy allies, hostile neutrals, malignant Fortune, ugly surprises, awful miscalculations—all take their seats at the Council Board. . . . Always remember, however sure you are that you can easily win, that there would not be a war if the other man did not think he also had a chance.[6]

The standards for determining whether or not a war is just are basically unworkable.

Reconciling the Eagle and the Dove

To where have we come? What can we say now about Christian obligations to Christ and Caesar in relation to foreign policy?

First, while government in general is ordained by God, a mandate from heaven cannot be applied to all governments and regimes. Surely the rise of Stalin in Russia and Hitler in Germany demonstrates that. Also how then could any soldier fight any country without fighting God?

Nations also change as times and circumstances change. The nature of specific governments is developed by heritage and culture as well as by the designs of men and their responses to particular pressing problems. The Depression of the 1930s was a worldwide phenomenon, but responses and policies to deal with it differed widely among governments.

In short, governments change, sometimes dramatically and radically, sometimes slowly and incrementally; but change they do. The American government today, for example, is vastly different from that envisioned by the Founding Fathers in 1789. The rise of industrialization, the centralization of power during the Civil War and the two world wars, the expansion of government activities under the New Deal and Great Society—these have greatly altered the American government in practice. Jefferson's ideals are retained and proclaimed by Democrat and Republican alike, but his ideals are embodied in the free electoral process and republican institutions, not in limited government and agrarian society. This all means that one cannot assume a constant presence of God's holy blessings on all governments for all times.

Second, the principalities and powers of evil exist in this world and can take control of a nation. Hence, one must recognize that the possibility exists for a government's policy or actions to be immoral and not permissible for participation by Christians.

Third, we have seen multiple and ambiguous perspectives being held by Christians on foreign policy. Foreign policy can appear meaningless and war never worth the cost of the death and destruction that inevitably occurs.

For centuries poets have written bitterly about the waste and horror of ruined lives, disfigured bodies and destroyed plans caused by wars. Yet other men who fought and bled in wars have seen deep personal meaning for themselves in terms of their discipline, bravery and willingness to jeopardize their lives for their country and fellow citizens. Some Christians see the requirements of foreign policy and war leading to greater technological and scientific developments and so a better life in peacetime. Others see a discrepancy and danger between the desire to protect the nation and the militarization growing out of the reliance on weapons to protect the nation and resolve disputes. Some Christians see a grand design of God unfolding in the developments of world politics and find meaning and comfort in that perspective. Others question the ability to see clearly and authoritatively where, how and in what manner and direction God is moving in historical events.

Most of the sins dealt with by the Scriptures are those of personal choice regarding one's own life. Sexual license, drunkenness, lying—these are plainly identified and prohibited. But the Scriptures are not an unambiguous sourcebook of foreign policy ethics. Certain concerns of the Christian life are clear—love, compassion, service, justice—but how they are applied to the world of nations has been subject to disagreement.

That diversity of opinion is useful. It promotes increased reliance on God's particular will for our personal lives, with our own capabilities, in our specific situations. Being personal, the Christian faith must be tolerant of the opinions of other Christians in this area of morality and foreign policy. Christians are one at the point of the cross, but go forth to serve in various capacities as the Scriptures and Holy Spirit lead.

Without certainty and permanence in international politics, and lacking a manual of foreign policy ethics to serve as a substitute pope, Christians must rely on their divinely led rationality. Dogmatism and ideology in either sphere is inappropriate. Rationality apart from the Scriptures and guidance of the Holy Spirit is merely cunning craftiness.

Recognizing the importance of tolerance and rationality, Christians should guard against being judgmental of divergent opinions. Political issues are emotional issues, and while Christians can and will disagree over them, they should not become divided over them. Rather than accumulating "proof texts" and asserting authority and righteousness in pursuit of unity of view, Christians should discuss their perspectives. They should weigh the views of each other to insure their own views are not unbalanced. And they should seek to find ways to work collectively, though perhaps in different ways, to advance conditions of love, peace, reconciliation, compassion, justice.

The diversity of opinion should not obscure the fact that some policies can be evil and that moral concerns and responsibilities of Christians should not be isolated and compartmentalized from foreign policy. Given the values of Christians, it should be possible to identify the clearly immoral actions and policies.

The criteria employed in marking out those boundaries should include policy goals, methods and consequences. Goals must be included because policies cannot be allowed to serve to deify a nation, a leader or a people. A false god must not be established. Additionally, some goals are unnecessary or unimportant, not worth the costs of being pursued. The goals must not be opposed to what the Christian holds valuable—communion with God and community with people of worth, value and dignity.

Methods of pursuing political policy are important. They may become so demonic that they negate the justice that originally motivated the policy. There must be some restraint in the type of methods used and in the intensity of their use. How much restraint is determined by the value of the goals pursued and by the consequences that result.

Consequences are important. Leaders can face choices that have no desirable options, no good answers, no pure goals, no nonlethal means. It is then that the consequences of various options become an important criterion for judgment and evaluation. Ignoring consequences can cause needless death and destruction.

Two principles that reflect this criterion are political prudence and strategic proportionality. Political prudence relates to the goals of a regime's policy. It specifies that a regime should not attempt goals that the nation is unable to achieve or that are unattainable in the reality of world politics. The blood, sweat and tears of the people, the resources and honor of the nation and the public confidence in the regime and government are not wasted. The sacrifices remain within rational bounds.

Strategic proportionality relates to the methods and consequences of a policy. It dictates that a regime should use methods that insure that the policy has a reasonable chance of success. Costs should not outweigh the benefits. Destruction should not be out of proportion to what is necessary. And noncombatants should be spared. This principle helps preserve rationality in operations, helps minimize physical and emotional destruction and tragedy, and helps maintain a perspective amenable to justice and humanity.

Political prudence and strategic proportionality are workable principles for identifying (and also avoiding) immoral policies. If prudence is ignored and goals are absolutized, eliminating all restraints, the result is death and destruction that: (a) is on such a wide scale as to constitute an obvious rejection of Christian and even humanist ideals of the value of man; (b) unnecessary for the establishment or for the protection of a humane community, a community that allows for the sovereignty of God, the recognition of the equality of man and the expression of such values as love, compassion and mercy; and (c) is carried out exclusively in pursuit of the glorification of a nation, leader or ideology.

This situation is seen in the policies of Hitler in Poland and Russia in World War 2. There was widespread destruction, torture and killings carried out in those countries against ordinary, noncombatant citizens. That policy was not necessary for the *safety* of Germany, but it was for the *expansion* of Germany and the *glorification* of Hitler and the German race. Everything about that policy in Eastern Europe offends our Christian consciences.

If strategic proportionality is ignored, then the results are actions, weapons and strategies which: (a) become exceedingly destructive to humans and their ability to provide for basic needs, like food, shelter and clothing; (b) are incapable of achieving the stated or intended goal, no matter how just the objective may be; and (c) are employed against a nation which poses no immediate physical threat. Such a combination of elements does not rule out military aid to another nation under attack if that attack can be effectively repelled or deterred from reoccurring. It also does not automatically preclude the use of weapons of mass destruction against a real physical threat. What is immoral is the use of excessive means. These might be employed because of a loss of control by leaders or the frustration of leaders over their inability to achieve their objective.

Wars and other foreign actions are not undertaken for their own sakes but to achieve certain purposes. And those purposes, assuming they are acceptable, must always determine the selection of means and the extent of application of those means. When that connection breaks down in operations against a nation that does not pose a threat or danger, and extreme destruction is being carried out against noncombatants and nonmilitary targets, such a set of circumstances is immoral.

Using the principles of prudence and proportionality is not a perfect solution. It does not always provide easy answers. It is characterized in part by a limitation or minimization of the scope of activities that can be called immoral. There are dangers in too free an application of moral judgment in political issues. It can lead to endless debates and arguments among Christians, which is detrimental if it generates hostilities in the Family of God or if it diverts Christians from their primary purposes. It can lead to diminished influence with the world if we "waste our substance on riotous moralizing."[7] It can cause us to use God to justify our predispositions and political biases without serious searching to insure our attitudes are in harmony with God. When we do apply moral judgments, we should do so humbly. Politics, especially world politics, are sometimes moved by great historical forces, the nature of which we only dimly perceive if at all. Carl Sandburg said of Abraham Lincoln,

> In the mixed shame and blame of the immense wrongs of two crashing civilizations, often with nothing to say, he said nothing, slept not at all, and on occasions he was seen to weep in a way that made weeping appropriate, decent, majestic.[8]

But at the same time there can come a time when we must say, "This far and no further." For a Christian, there are bounds to what belongs to Caesar. I have attempted to make clear where those bounds are.

Finally, this reconciliation of the Eagle and the Dove is

characterized by a latitude in values. It posits human life as a value to be protected from wasteful destruction. It permits recognition of the necessity of national interest. It allows for national action on behalf of the protection of other nations far away.

Questions and Answers

Q. You seem to have said that we shouldn't love our country, that it is unchristian to be patriotic.

A. No. The love of country is natural and desirable, and so long as we live in this world it should be developed if the nation is deserving. What I tried to say was that patriotism can serve various needs. One must beware lest a false god is created or a false criterion of Christianity be established.

I am concerned that the church not confuse loyalty to a state with a commandment of God. Churches and pastors receive special tax concessions, national songs are included in hymnals, the American flag is flown from many church platforms—all these are intended to reflect the church's gratitude for freedom of worship in this country. But they also generate an assumption that love of country is a Christian duty. Love of country is a good and desirable attribute, but it is not a specifically Christian attribute. Paul and Peter exhorted obedience to government, but they nowhere ever exhorted love for country. The nation and government are secular institutions, just like football games and fire engines and steam trains, all of which are the objects of special love for some people, but none of which is particularly Christian.

Q. Shouldn't we favor any war against Communists since they are godless and oppose Christianity? Isn't that also a responsibility of America?

A. I don't agree. I don't see value in justifying action against communist nations on Christian grounds. Government action against such nations, regardless of the government's motives, may be supported by you for religious reasons as your own personal reasons for support of that action. But there are a number of problems with forcing nations into Christian and non-Christian categories.

For one thing, it makes you into a crusader, demanding conflict. And if peace in this world is based on a balance of power and the development of international ties, you will end up opposing government efforts to relax international tensions and reach agreements with communist nations. Such agreements are compromises with evil.

It is also difficult to determine just where particular nations should be placed in categories of pro-Christian and anti-Christian. Usually nations are not one hundred per cent of either. And American Christians have the curious habit, though actually I am sure it is common to all nations, of seeing evil rampant throughout the land, with corruption in government, crime in the streets, distortion in the media, sensualism in advertising and disrespect in the schools. Yet at the same time they see America as God's tool for defending Christianity around the world and opposing evil in other lands.

Now I do believe that America has done a praiseworthy job in resisting the spread of communism. But I am reluctant to see America as God's chosen people because of that. And I cannot shut my eyes to the compromises with tyranny in noncommunist nations in order to do so. Senator Fulbright may be wrong about many things, but he is dead right when he talks about the danger of an "arrogance of power" as Americans confuse their nation's power with virtue.

Q. Well, I say "God bless America."

A. And I do, too. I want God's blessing on this land and not his judgment. I want God to work in and through us for the good of the world and the building of his kingdom. I invoke his blessing but I don't assume myself to be God's tool because I am an American. I want his guidance for the nation, but I don't believe he is so locked into identity with America that the nation will be forever pure or that he will not judge and punish us for any possible present or future evil the nation does. There is a difference between saying "God bless America" as a request, and saying it as a means of justifying ourselves and repudiating any criticism.

Basic Readings

Bennett, John Coleman. *Foreign Policy in Christian Perspective*. New York: Charles Scribner's Sons. 1966. Bennett writes from the realist position.

Hostetler, Paul. Ed. *Perfect Love and War*. Nappanee, Indiana: Evangel Press. 1974. This book is a compilation of papers and responses presented at a Seminar on Christian Holiness and the Issues of War and Peace.

Kaplan, Morton. *Strategic Thinking and Its Moral Implications*. The University of Chicago Press. 1973.

Kennan, George. *Foreign Policy and Christian Conscience*. Philadelphia: American Friends Service Committee. 1959.

Long, Edward LeRoy. *War and Conscience in America*. Philadelphia: Westminster Press. A good introduction to the general categories of religious thought on the issue of war.

MacGregor, G. H. C. *The New Testament Basis of Pacifism*. New York: Fellowship of Reconciliation. 1954.

Mayer, Peter. Ed. *The Pacifist Conscience*. New York: Holt, Rinehart and Winston. 1966.

Ramsey, Paul. *The Just War: Force and Political Responsibility*. New York: Charles Scribner's Sons. 1968.

Potter, Ralph. *War and Moral Discourse*. Richmond, Virginia: John Knox Press. 1970.

Tucker, Robert. *The Just War: A Study in Contemporary American Doctrine*. Baltimore: The Johns Hopkins Press. 1960.

copyright 1969 by Herblock in The Washington Post

"Watch those bread crumbs—bread costs money."

56415

IV
SWORDS
& SPEARS

*"They shall beat their swords into plowshares,
and their spears into pruning hooks;
nation shall not lift up sword against nation,
neither shall they learn war any more.
O house of Jacob, come, let us walk in the
light of the LORD."
Isaiah 2:4-5*

Swords and spears were not unknown to Israel. Subjected for a time in Egypt with swords and spears, Israel used them to conquer the Promised Land and today uses them to protect itself from foreign threats. That history is similar to the history of many nations, including America.

Organized warfare has existed since people settled in organized communities. But for almost as long people have longed for the fulfillment of Isaiah's prophecy that one day the world would turn from the works of war to concentrate on the work for a better life.

Waging war with today's swords and spears raises the human stakes of conflict and confronts the Christian's conscience with many new issues. The use of missiles, bombers and long-range cannon means the enemy is not seen

Lincoln Christian College

(and neither is the tragedy of his suffering) and the destruction of noncombatants is unavoidable. Issues also arise from the Defense Department's deep involvement in the everyday life of the American society. To understand better the moral implications of the use of swords and spears, Christians need to understand how decisions for their use are made and how the Pentagon's involvement in society affects the attitudes and values of the American people.

There is no hope that the world's people will rise up in a fit of spontaneous euphoria and turn their tanks and cannons into farm reapers. But there is a hope that military agreements can be made that will lessen the costs and dangers of modern weapons. America and Russia are currently involved in Strategic Arms Limitation Talks (SALT Talks), and on those talks ride the hopes of millions of people. Can the nations themselves bring about Isaiah's prophecy? Should Christians automatically support such efforts and oppose the military establishment as contrary to the teachings of Scripture?

The Department of Defense

A helpful starting place for understanding today's Defense Department is the military establishment as it existed through World War 2: two separate and independent services—the Army and the Navy—with their own perspectives on strategy, budgetary priorities, strategic threat and operational roles. The growing independence of the Army Air Corps with its own perspectives as well as the emergence of a distinct identity and role for the Marine Corps as the Navy's amphibious assault force further aggravated this lack of unity.

This parochialism created severe handicaps in reaching agreement on fundamental issues of strategy in World War 2 and caused a reluctance by both services to participate in a subordinate role in the strategy and campaigns of the other. The obvious weakness of this arrangement was compounded when it was necessary to cooperate with an ally who had different strategic designs. The war ended, therefore, with a widespread determination to create some new way to coordinate future planning and operations.

The issue crystallized when the Air Corps struggled with the other services over its share of governmental funds and over its future role and status. At issue among the services was not just past traditions and future cooperation, but perhaps the very existence of the Army and Navy themselves, for the atomic bomb appeared in the late 1940s to be a weapon capable of decisively ending wars without armies or navies.

The Army, undergoing rapid demobilization, advocated unification of the military services into a single military department, an arrangement that would formalize and guarantee its equality in budgetary competition with the congressionally popular Navy and Air Force. The Navy opposed unification and advocated a hierarchy of coordinating committees among three independent services representing the three battle theaters of ground, air and sea. Admiral King, opposing absorption or subordination of the Navy in a new military department argued, "If the Navy's welfare is one of the prerequisites to the nation's welfare—and I sincerely believe that to be the case—any step that is not good for the Navy is not good for the nation."[1] The Air Corps, possessing the vehicles for delivering atomic weapons, perceived a secure identity and status in either arrangement.

The National Security Act of 1947 generally resolved this controversy. Subsequent modifications of that Act concentrated greater power in the Secretary of Defense at the expense of the military services.

The Department of Defense is an executive department managing three subordinate military departments—Army, Navy and Air Force. It is a civilian department. It integrates policies, provides personnel, equipment and facilities, and undertakes research, training and intelligence operations. This structure perpetuates service identities and interservice competition. The Department achieves some unity while the interservice rivalry prevents the Department from becoming dominated by the military.

Within the Department is the military command structure. Except for the Secretary of Defense, the civilian members of the Department do not participate in the direction of military operations. The command of the armed forces flows from the president through the Secretary of Defense and the Joint Chiefs of Staff to field commanders. This dual structure (civilian and military) is a major characteristic of the Department.

At the apex of each military service is a Chief of Staff responsible for advising the Secretary of Defense on military affairs, for planning, developing and executing programs of his service, and for determining the weapon requirements of his service. These three Chiefs, together with a Chairman, collectively comprise the Joint Chiefs of Staff (JCS). The Commandant of the Marine Corps is included as an equal member whenever the topic before the JCS involves the Corps. The JCS acts as a military staff for strategic planning, for control of combat forces, and for offering advice to the president, the Secretary of Defense and the National Security Council. The planning and command activities do not make the JCS equivalent to a General Staff as existed in Germany in World War 1 since its authority is not independent of the president and the secretary.

In giving advice to the president the JCS takes into account political, economic and psychological factors rather than purely military factors and is directed to advise on broad aspects of U.S. foreign policy and not be just a group of military specialists. But there are important weaknesses with the JCS as an advisory institution. The Chiefs are supposed to be both representatives of their services and neutral, objective military analysts. As a collegial body they have found agreement among themselves on matters of priorities, force levels and strategy difficult to achieve. On major issues such as size and composition of forces, strategic concepts and the budget, the JCS has repeatedly deadlocked. Not only does this reduce the ability of the Department to establish unity of purpose and operation in U.S. forces—except when the JCS reaches agreement by simply asking for a budget large enough to finance all their divergent plans—but it also slows the ability of the JCS to react to a crisis.

The Secretary of Defense exercises his authority over the Department through the three Secretaries of the military departments and through his Office of the Secretary of Defense. The latter, comprising nine Assistant Secretaries and assorted other office managers, was used by Secretary Robert McNamara to assert his control over military policy. In this way he achieved greater unity in U.S. military policy and forces than since the Second World War.

This new degree of unity came through the consolidation of parallel functions of the services into single offices, such as the Defense Intelligence Agency, the Defense Supply Agency and the Defense Contract Audit Agency. Further unity came through the development of consolidated military functions and the introduction of managerial techniques like the Planning-Programming-Budgeting System and Cost Effectiveness. Also, staffs like the Office of International Security Affairs provided an alternative source of information and analysis for reviewing the requests and policies of the JCS.

This civilian participation in the Office of International Security Affairs and the Office of Systems Analysis can be crucial to realistic policy-making in military affairs. It can overcome the parochial recommendations of the services and the reluctance of service officers to present independent judgments that might lead to criticisms of established policies and so jeopardize their careers. Civilian involvement can also maintain a grasp on the rampant technological change and its implications for strategy and forces.

Strategy and weapons development continues to be built around the strategic functions introduced by McNamara rather than around military services or theaters. The result is that strategy is more than a combination of each service's independently developed plans, and weapons development is tied to integrated plans. These functions and the weapon systems they involve are:

Strategic Offense—the capacity to assure the destruction of any threatening nuclear power, through the use of nuclear weapons delivered by heavy bombers, intercontinental ballistic missiles and a missile-armed submarine fleet.

Strategic Defense—the defense of the North American continent through surveillance and warning systems, interceptor forces and civil defense programs.

General Purpose—the capacity to undertake large-scale conventional, limited, unconventional or counter-revolutionary operations. The forces involved are Army divisions and artillery, naval fleets and Marine Corps, and aircraft wings.

Airlift and Sealift—the capacity to transport men and material and weapons to potential and actual battlefields or overseas bases. The forces include transport, cargo and tanker planes, ships and helicopters.

Identification and development of forces necessary to implement these functions are carried out through the Planning-Programming-Budgeting System. In the Planning stage, the JCS develops a Joint Strategic Objectives Plan (JSOP) which incorporates the recommendations of the services and the JCS collectively regarding strategy, forces and programs for the next four years. Planning also involves identifying alternative program units—integrated combinations of men, equipment and installations—to achieve the proposals of the JSOP. This planning is done within the strategic and fiscal guidance from the Office of the Secretary. A program unit like Attack Carriers incorporates not just the carriers but also the men, the attack and defensive aircraft, and the defensive destroyers that must accompany the carrier and the bases.

Budgeting involves determining the total costs of the program—developmental costs, investment costs and operating costs. With this information on goals, alternative program units and total costs of alternatives, the Office of Systems Analysis (in the McNamara era) applied Cost Effectiveness criteria in selecting program units for acceptance and recommendation to Congress. Cost Effectiveness meant comparing alternative program units on the basis of their cost and what they could achieve, so effectiveness was maximized and cost minimized.

There were many critics of Cost Effectiveness, both within and outside the military, and in some cases it appears that McNamara used Cost Effectiveness as a justification for, rather than a foundation for, his decisions. The Nixon Administration reorganized and downgraded the Office of Systems Analysis into the Defense Program Analysis and Evaluation Staff, gave more authority to the JCS in program selection, and moved the final decisions on recommendations for the president to a committee of the National Security Council in the White House.

Another major characteristic of the Department is the acceptance of civilian control despite the strong commitment of the Officer Corps to professionalism as a departmental and personal goal. A fundamental reason for this acceptance of civilian control is the absence of a military aristocracy in this country.

There are several reasons for this. First, the Civil War ended the plantation system and its potential for developing into a military aristocracy. Second, the involvement of Congress in the appointment of cadets to West Point assures a wide geographical and social distribution. Third, the military itself has recently adopted management techniques like systems analysis and operations research. It has also broadened outside contacts through formal exchange programs between itself and other civilian agencies. At the same time, however, military officers have increasingly been called upon by presidents to hold administrative positions in other agencies, a reflection of the fact that modern warfare requires that the highest commanders also be effective administrators.

In all of this it must be remembered that the military is not a monolith of consensus. Separate services with separate traditions and career patterns and the nature of the budgetary process lead to inherent and automatic competition and conflict between the services.

The concept of the "military mind" has some basis in reality. The military values planning and doctrine. It controls power of enormous impact. And it sees itself as the defender of the nation. Also, as in any social organization with a distinct identity, individuals must be socialized into that organization's culture before being allowed to rise to offices of greater authority. Some officers in the military, as in other organizations, are zealots for organizational or personal reasons, and they develop an attitude not unlike the priesthood or ministry in serving a cause. But the socialization process does not kill all individuality and commitment. As in most large organizations, the highest levels of authority and responsibility in the military have a much broader perception of the relationship of the military to foreign policy than do lower levels. The military mind at these highest levels does not seem markedly different from the legal or business mind.

The Department of Defense at Home
Despite its principal concern with foreign affairs, the Department is deeply involved in American society. Its expenditures for supplies and payroll can dominate a local economy. The existence of a military base or facility in a community inflates housing prices, overcrowds schools, and strains medical, entertainment and public services. And after a community has made the necessary adjustments, it can be dealt a depressing if not lethal blow if the Pentagon decides to abolish or relocate the base for budgetary reasons.

The previous draft system and the present volunteer recruitment system operate differently on different segments of the population. But it is still a tool of social
change and development. The draft inducted fewer men
from the bottom of the social scale because of educational
and medical deficiencies and fewer men from the top of
the society because of educational and occupational defer-
ments. Yet for those men from the lower end of society that
were inducted, the military acted as a vehicle for basic and
vocational education, providing many of them with an
educational "second chance." The Volunteer Army has
led to a great increase in the number of blacks and under-
educated in the military and to a drop in the number of
men available to serve in hospitals and similar institutions
as an alternative to the draft. The Indian Health Service, for
example, is faced with extinction because it relied on recruiting medical doctors who wanted an approved alternative to military service.

The services also have an impact on racial attitudes.
Prolonged contact under conditions of relative equality
and high interdependence reduces racial prejudice among
whites. It also affects the blacks, for their experience with
relative equality in the service increases their demands for
the same equality when they re-enter civilian society.

Financially, the Department spends about sixty per cent
of its nonpayroll budget on materials for which there is no
significant commercial market, creating huge corporations
that are heavily dependent upon, if not mere appendages
of, the military. Additionally, a profit percentage is guaranteed to defense contractors, and much of the plant and
equipment for the contractors is built and financed by the
government, creating a no-risk situation for the corporations and reducing the need to economize. An employment linkage has also been developed between the services and their contractors, whereby large numbers of re-
tiring military officers move to high positions in defense
industries and top level civilians move from their firms to

the Pentagon and back again to their firms. The results of all of this have been the destruction of capitalism among defense-related corporations, constant "cost overruns," and continuing fears and charges that the interlocking ties lead to conflicts of interest which affect decisions on approving new weapons systems and awarding contracts.

Departmental spending affects the economy in another way. Its requirement for constant improvements and innovations in weapons technology has led to large-scale financing of research. This has contributed important domestic benefits but has also subsidized the size and prestige of the natural sciences over the social sciences and humanities in colleges and universities, and contributed to the belief that science and technology can solve our social problems. This funding system has also created a large scientific establishment dependent upon government defense contracts. This creates the danger of massive unemployment during periods of spending reductions as well as a community of scholars which must avoid controversial issues. The scientific estate, assuming that weaponry is a way of life, disregards the goals and uses to which its work is contributing. In fact, according to a major scientific publication,

> An engineer who has built his career around the weapons acquisition process is tugged at by considerations that do not affect the typical citizen. He has a vested interest in any state of affairs that guarantees a continuing demand for his own expertise. There is also that inescapable characteristic of the engineer—the strong desire to see if a design really works.[2]

In short, defense spending in the civilian society can lead to subtle demands for approval and support of military policies. Other factors lead to similar pressures.

The large veterans associations actively propagate a certain view of the world. Their older members tend to romanticize and exaggerate their own military experiences and loyalties, leading to unrealistic expectations from the younger generation. The presence of the military in parades, county fairs, observances of national holidays, and on recruiting signs and billboards make the military the most visible symbol of the national government next to the Post Office. The uniforms, brass decorations, and precision marching and formations create an image of authority in an increasingly permissive society and evoke the emotions of pride, tradition and trust. The flags and drums and standard content of speeches recall traditions, glorified history and form standards of judgment on foreign and sometimes domestic affairs.

It is upon such factors as these, rather than on the merits of issues, that the perspectives and decisions of the military are accepted by many Americans. They also lead many Christians either to compartmentalize issues of religion and war, suspending the application of moral standards upon the military, or to see the conservative aspects of religion (the place of authority, doctrine and heritage) reflected in these public images of the military. Support of the military becomes a by-product of religious commitment.

This overview of the structure, operations and decision-making processes of the Department of Defense means that Christian citizens must recognize that military decisions are made on the basis of more than pure rationality. There are deep strains of service and career self-interest in policy-making arguments and decisions. Additionally, while generals and admirals below the JCS level consider themselves and their decisions as the only bulwark against foreign policy disasters, the Christian must remember that national military policy is only one aspect of U.S. foreign policy, one option, the effectiveness of which varies according to circumstances. But it is an aspect that is appealing for its virility and dynamism opposed to so-called "soft-headed" alternatives. Also, the Pentagon is aided in mobilizing attitudes of support for itself and its policies by its emotional symbols and economic power.

Finally, the Christian needs to recognize that nationalism, patriotism and loyalty are not synonymous with automatic support of any and all budget requests of the Pentagon. Issues of policy and weapon procurement are hotly debated within the Pentagon and the executive branch, so an individual citizen's disagreement with a proposed policy or adopted policy is not necessarily subversive, arrogant or inappropriate.

Conventional War

War in today's world can be classified into the three categories of conventional, nuclear and limited. The twentieth century has seen the emergence of wars that encompass the whole globe. But large-scale wars have occurred since the Middle Ages—the Hundred Years War, the Thirty Years War, the War of the Spanish Succession and the Napoleonic Wars. These wars with their twentieth-century counterparts have formed the typical image of war, and they have several characteristics in common: *stakes*— they all involve an attempt to change the basic power structure of the world, usually by conquering and dominating the European continent; *time*—these wars usually last several years; *forces*—every type of non-nuclear weapon available is used because of the immense stakes involved; *strategy*—commanders aim at the annihilation of enemy forces in a huge bloody, climactic battle.

The strategy of annihilation was developed by Napoleon. Both sides employed this strategy in World War 1, but the earlier development of the machine gun, the raising of mass armies too large to be beaten in a single stroke and the economic resilience of an industrial economy ruined the strategy. Battles degenerated into repeated frontal assaults with no triumphant climax. The result was bloody attrition and mutual exhaustion.

Proponents of air forces, including Billy Mitchell in this country, argued that this new horror of deadlocked war could be broken by the use of air power against an enemy's industrial and population centers. The destruction and terror coming from a hailstorm of bombs would return decisiveness to war by breaking the enemy's morale and will to fight. The Germans used that strategy against England and the English and Americans used it against the Germans in World War 2. Both sides mounted massive bomber fleets and constant air raids. Both sides failed. Air war became indecisive because antiaircraft weapons were more effective and enemy morale more resolute than expected.

Consequently, World War 2 degenerated into the kind of struggle that characterized the American Civil War—a remorseless battling until one side was finally worn down and overwhelmed by the side with greater resources. It was a dirty, rotten type of war. Just as General Sherman marched to the sea leaving a swath of destruction in his wake, so the Allies bombed and fought and struggled ahead, finally entering a completely destroyed Germany. As Sherman said, "War is hell." The losses in World War 2 were staggering.

Yet, what was the alternative—European submission to Hitler and Japanese control of the seas? Surely once the war had begun there was no alternative but to fight it rather than submit to those results. If any war fits the criteria of prudence and proportionality mentioned in chapter three, it was the Second World War. Whether or not it could have been prevented by a wiser foreign policy earlier is another question. At this point we simply want to note that World War 2 reveals that at times war is both an inescapable fact of life and a necessity for a nation.

However justifiable these wars may appear, they all raise enormous moral issues. World wars can cause a mobilization and hardening of purposes. As the intensity and destructiveness of the war increases, the goals and purposes of the war take on greater emotional significance. That in turn justifies further expansion in intensity and an increase in destructiveness, and the war tends to jerk out of the bounds of restraint and control.

World wars create new attitudes toward and images of people which the Christian must be able to recognize and then neutralize. The pressures of war tend to mold an image of the enemy as a characterization of evil. The enemy is not just wrong or selfish; he is evil, terrible, malevolent and a fit object of hatred. The tendency to depersonalize the enemy also exists, to view him as subhuman, a creature to be killed with no feeling of guilt or remorse.

But remember the words of Christ: "Love your enemies and pray for those who persecute you" (Mt. 5:44). Remember also humility, for without the grace of God you might very well be just as unjust as the enemy.

Remember too that the enemy, like you, is motivated by loyalty and patriotism and by his belief that his government is right and is fighting for protection from you. And if you think that his belief in his government's policy is self-delusion, then remember that you too *can* be deluded. So search your own motivations.

You may find that he is deluded, that he is participating in an obvious case of aggression. The Russian commanders prohibited their troops from talking with Czechoslovakian citizens during and after the 1968 Russian invasion of Czechoslovakia. They knew how difficult it would be for Russian troops to rationalize their invasion to Czechoslovakian citizens who were painting swastikas on Russian tanks.

When you check your motivations you may also find that you have been deluded. Many Americans felt that way in the 1890s when, after supporting the Spanish-American War in order to free Cuba from Spanish colonial rule, they found that the war ended with Cuba, the Philippines and Puerto Rico as American protectorates. In the public park of a certain American city I have seen a statue dedicated to the unknown soldiers who gave their lives in the Philippine Insurrection. What was the Philippine Insurrection? It was the effort of Philippine patriots to throw off the

American occupation, an effort resisted by the American military. It resulted in 1,500 Philippino casualties and 272 American casualties. This was at the end of a war the American public thought was designed to free captive peoples not simply to replace Spanish occupation with American occupation.

When you search your own motivations and those of your own nation, you may find something else—that both you and your enemy are caught in the grip of historical forces and social pressures that are not fully understood and that appear to be out of control, propelling men and nations toward unwanted and deadly actions. And in the midst of those tides of events the locations of right and wrong appear obscured. That is a frightening time. One wishes that all momentous international conflicts were as clear-cut as World War 2 when, even though England and France were not free of the taint of colonialism, the difference between those nations and the Nazi forces was so immense that the question of which side to support was obvious.

Yet not all conflicts are that clear. Remember in our own history the words of President Abraham Lincoln in his Second Inaugural Address:

On the occasion corresponding to this four years ago, all thoughts were anxiously directed to an impending civil war. All dreaded it—all sought to avert it. While the inaugural address was being delivered from this place, devoted altogether to saving the Union without war, insurgent agents were in the city seeking to destroy it without war—seeking to dissolve the Union, and divide effects, by negotiation. Both parties depreciated war; but one of them would make war rather than let the nation survive; and the other would accept war rather than let it perish. And the war came....

Neither party expected for the war the magnitude or the duration which it has already attained. Neither anticipated that the cause of the conflict might cease with, or even before, the conflict itself should cease. Each looked for an easier triumph, and a result less fundamental and astonishing. Both read the same Bible and pray to the same God; and each invokes his aid against the other. It may seem strange that any men should dare to ask a just God's assistance in wringing their bread from the sweat of other men's faces; but let us judge not, that we be not judged. The prayers of both could not be answered—that of neither has been answered fully.

What then should one do in such a situation? In lines that will live as long as this nation lives, Lincoln answers that we should act, "with malice toward none, with charity for all; with firmness in the right, as God gives us to see the right. . . ."

There is yet another set of attitudes affected by war, those attitudes that determine what kind of men and actions will be called honorable and meritorious. In war the rewards of honor and praise go to men who are successful in their job of killing the enemy. But what happens to those men who are rewarded by their government for being aggressive, domineering and deadly, and then come home and are expected to be law abiding citizens, tender and loving husbands, humble and compassionate churchmen?

One must beware that his nation does not succumb and let the reward for patriotic heroism become so all consuming in the nation's value system that power and force are glorified. The German nation was built out of "blood and thunder" and in the process it became a nation typified by the Prussian soldier. That national self-image carried down through the 1930s and made the bloody policies of Hitler easier.

The Christian must be careful that the world of war does not mold his image of the hero. The Christian may be a warrior, even a professional career soldier, but his posture toward life in general and toward other men in particular must grow out of the Holy Spirit's presence in his life and not out of his vocation as a fighter.

Nuclear War

Albert Einstein suggested in a letter to President Franklin Roosevelt that a new kind of weapon could be built, one using atomic processes and capable of fantastic destruction. Roosevelt understood the significance of the letter and directed that work begin at once on developing that weapon. A massive undertaking was begun in an effort called The Manhattan Project. This led to the bomb that was dropped and killed 80,000 people at Hiroshima on August 6, 1945. Thus was born the atomic bomb and the future possibility of a nuclear war.

There are three important features of nuclear weapons that we must understand. One feature is their magnitude of destruction. The most powerful conventional bombs used in World War 2 were "blockbusters" of about one ton of trinitrotoluene (T.N.T.). The Hiroshima bomb equaled 20,000 tons or 20 kilitons of T.N.T. and alone leveled most of the city and killed 80,000 residents. In 1955 America had nuclear weapons of 20,000,000 tons or 20 megatons of T.N.T.

What would happen to war if each nation used multitudes of 20 megaton bombs? It would become possible, for the first time, to not just conquer a nation after a long and strenuous war but to obliterate it in a few minutes. For example, with a combination of bombing, chemical and gaseous weapons and large-scale invasion, the U.S. could have exterminated the population of the Japanese islands, 80 million, without nuclear weapons. We had no reason to do so and would not have had the will for such an enormous mass execution. Yet it is probable that we will destroy 200 million Russians if a nuclear war breaks out between the United States and Russia, for such destruction would be almost automatic and instantaneous.

Thus it is now possible and probably militarily imperative to do what would have been unimaginable in 1945. And, unfortunately, a radical increase in the number of deaths, such as from 80,000 to 200,000,000 dulls, rather than sharpens, peoples' appreciation of the enormity of the destruction, and their sense of sympathy with the victims.

A second feature of nuclear weapons is radiation and radioactive fallout. Radiation is the emission of highly charged energy rays that can penetrate matter. These rays are deadly. Many of the pioneer scientists working with X-rays and other radioactive materials suffered burns that would not heal. They often had to have the spread of these wounds and the threat of a lingering and torturous death arrested by amputation. Others, like Madame Curie, who discovered various radioactive substances, died from the resulting leukemia.

Radiation also damages human reproductive organs which leads to defective children. The explosion of a nuclear weapon digs up and hurls giant amounts of dirt and debris into the air and makes that debris radioactive. After being carried across the earth's surface by winds this radioactive fallout settles back to the earth, bringing its poison of radiation to nations not even near the fighting states. This was one of the major issues at stake in nuclear testing in the 1950s and early 1960s. Those tests also produced a band of radiation in the atmosphere far above the surface of the earth that severely damaged orbiting satellites that flew through it.

In short, the magnitude of destruction is amplified by radiation and fallout. It expands in scope through the new kinds of disease and death it brings. It expands in time through damage to heredity. And it expands in geography through traveling fallout.

A third feature is the delivery of nuclear weapons by missiles. We noted in chapter two that the significance of the development of intercontinental missiles is the inability of nations to defend against them. They fly too high and too fast. Thus nations lost their means to protect themselves when weapons were developed that could obliterate them.

What shall we say then? How shall we escape? And are these weapons so uniquely destructive that their existence and use are clearly immoral? Do we have any right to build and use large numbers of weapons that cannot only destroy us but our posterity as well?

It should first be noted that not all nuclear weapons are of the 20 megaton size. The U.S. arsenal includes some battlefield weapons of less size than that dropped in Japan and less than some of the larger conventional bombs. But that does not mean they could easily be used. The nuclear nations have maintained a "nuclear firebreak"—they distinguish between nuclear and non-nuclear weapons so that it is easier not to use large nuclear weapons if small ones have never been used either. And the longer they are not used the stronger grows the pressure not to use them. But once they begin to be used, they will be considered just another weapon and a major restraint on their use will have been eliminated.

Second, even though a nuclear war would be morally anathema so would a unilateral rejection of nuclear weapons which would leave us open to subjugation by a totalitarian dictator. If the existence of an American nuclear arsenal can prevent the United States and other nations from becoming part of a world slave farm or prison camp, which would also determine the destiny of our posterity, then such an arsenal should be built. Einstein and other American scientists worked on developing the atomic bomb because they knew Hitler's scientists were working to build one too, and they knew what would happen if Germany developed atomic bombs first.

Third, nuclear weapons serve another purpose besides being tools for fighting a war—preventing or deterring a war. Deterrence rests on the simple proposition that if a nation knows it will be destroyed even if it attacks first, there is no reason or incentive to attack. It would be suicide. A Second Strike nuclear force can prevent nuclear war.

The American nuclear arsenal is not just a "stockpile." It is designed to be a Second Strike military force, one that can ride out an attack and still strike back and assure the destruction of the aggressor. America puts its nuclear missiles in concrete silos below ground and on submarines roving around the world's oceans and has nuclear bombs carried by its Air Force bomber fleet. These three components cannot all be destroyed at once. The United States can so threaten an adversary with suicide that it will not attack.

But are we not inviting nuclear war to occur, whether by accident or irrationality or subversion or whatever, just by maintaining a nuclear arsenal? If nations have such weapons, will they not resort to them if a future crisis of major proportions develops?

The nations have undertaken so-called "Fail Safe" procedures to prevent wars by accident or subversion. Against an irrational dictator or "mad Caesar" there is no defense except deterrence. But as to the last question, whether or not the pressures and uncertainties operating in a crisis situation would force a resort to nuclear weapons, there is no answer. There is no way to know what kind of decisions will be made in the tense and emotion-laden atmosphere of a nuclear confrontation.

Probably the closest we have come to that point was in the 1962 Cuban Missile Crisis. At that time the Soviet leaders proclaimed that the American blockade of Cuba was pushing "mankind toward the abyss of a world nuclear-missile war." The pressures and uncertainties on the two world leaders were enormous, perhaps unbearable. General Maxwell Taylor, Chairman of the Joint Chiefs of Staff in 1962, has written about Premier Khrushchev:

> On the night of October 26, President Kennedy received that strange, disjointed letter from Khrushchev which has often been mentioned but never published. I would agree with those who have described it as the letter of a man either drunk or distraught, or both.... The lan-

guage of the letter caused me uneasiness, suggesting as
it did a disquieting instability on the part of the Soviet
leader whose rationality was so essential to world
peace.[3]

Robert Kennedy, close brother and defender of the president, wrote about the American leaders as the crisis
peaked:

> I think these few minutes were the time of gravest con-
> cern for the President. Was the world on the brink of a
> holocaust? Was it our error? A mistake? Was there some-
> thing further that should have been done? Or not done?
>
> His hand went up to his face and covered his mouth.
> He opened and closed his fist. His face seemed drawn,
> his eyes pained, almost gray. We stared at each other
> across the table. For a few fleeting seconds, it was al-
> most as though no one else was there and he was no
> longer the President.... We had come to the time of
> final decision. "We must expect that they will close
> down Berlin—make the final preparations for that,"
> the President said. I felt we were on the edge of a preci-
> pice with no way off.
>
> One thousand miles away, in the vast expanse of the
> Atlantic Ocean, the final decisions were going to be
> made in the next few minutes. President Kennedy had
> initiated the course of events, but he no longer had con-
> trol over them. He would have to wait—we would have
> to wait.[4]

The apprehension that we feel when reading these para-
graphs is compounded into consternation when we read
of the kind of advice the president was receiving at that
time. Robert Kennedy writes,

> On that fateful Sunday morning when the Russians
> answered they were withdrawing their missiles, it was
> suggested by one high military advisor that we attack
> Monday in any case. Another felt that we had in some
> way been betrayed.[5]

All of that sounds terribly disturbing. And it was. So much

so that it led the two world leaders to seek accommodation.

So if nuclear weapons are necessary, then the priority concern of the American government should be their control. In the 1960s the American leaders inaugurated measures and strategies to prevent any possible nuclear war from becoming an all-out war, such as: (1) A "hot line" between Moscow and Washington to facilitate communication and bargaining in a crisis or nuclear accident. (2) Procedures to prevent a single low-level commander from being able to fire nuclear weapons on his own. (3) Command of all U.S. nuclear weapons at home and overseas tightened and centralized to improve control and prevent any unauthorized firings. (4) A "counter-force" strategy announced which means in any future nuclear war, the U.S. would initially strike only military targets rather than population and other social targets, in effect holding those non-military targets "hostage," thereby increasing the incentive for an aggressor not to strike nonmilitary targets in the U.S.

If nuclear weapons cannot be rejected yet there is a danger they might be used in some future crisis, why not work out a disarmament treaty for the two super powers to sign? Should not disarmament be the goal of Christians? Is it not, by eliminating terror and destruction, a moral goal in itself?

If disarmament were feasible and wise, it would be a moral goal, but it is neither. Peace rests on the existence of a stable balance of power between nations. But power is not measured solely in terms of military equipment. It also includes the economic base of countries, as well as their population, morale, allies and technology. Given the large Russian Army, if the United States and Russia abolished their nuclear weapons, Russia would be the preponderant power in the world. If large-scale military equipment were abolished, China would be left preponderant. And anything that has been created once and destroyed can be built again. The only way to prevent nations from rebuilding their nuclear weapons in a crisis is to have eliminated all scientists from the earth, or at least destroyed their minds through lobotomies. Disarmament could only operate under a world government, and no nation is yet willing to trade the uncertainties of a possible future nuclear clash for the uncertainties of a world government that could become inhuman and tyrannical.

What is both possible and wise is a policy of seeking measures that limit nuclear weapons and reinforce deterrence at the same time. This is known as arms control and has been pursued by the United States and the Soviet Union.

Among the agreements that have been reached are the following: (1) The 1963 Nuclear Test Ban Treaty which prohibits nuclear tests in the atmosphere, thereby stopping the growth of radioactive substances in the air. (2) The 1968 Nuclear Non-Proliferation Treaty which prohibits nations with nuclear arms from giving them to nations without such armaments, thus reducing the odds of a nuclear war and preventing their being acquired by a "mad Caesar." (3) The 1971 Seabed Arms Control Treaty which prohibits the placement of weapons of mass destruction on the seabed, thereby eliminating a new arms race that could upset the military balance. (4) The 1972 SALT Agreement which put a freeze on the construction of new missiles. (5) The 1974 SALT Agreement which put a top limit on the number of missiles and nuclear warheads each nation could build and deploy.

Nuclear weapons are unavoidable at this time. For so long as they exist anywhere in the possession of an independent nation, they must be balanced by American nuclear forces operating as a deterrent force. Given that situation, then, we have seen the critical need to control them, to control their number, design, placement and proliferation.

But suppose deterrence fails. What then is the morality

of their use? Can thermonuclear war ever be just?

This issue poses an appalling dilemma. Some rational and moral justification for the existence of nuclear weapons can be found so long as they deter nuclear war and so protect the safety and well-being of the nation. But an opponent of the United States might come to believe America would never use its nuclear weapons in a war, and so that opponent might launch a drive of conquest over Europe or the Middle East. In that test of American credibility nuclear weapons might be used and in so doing destroy everything America had wanted to protect. Is nuclear war immoral but the threat of nuclear war justifiable?

To deal with this issue it is important to recognize that nuclear war does not have to be synonymous with nuclear annihilation. Nuclear weapons can be used at different levels of intensity. One writer has identified twenty-three levels of nuclear strikes.[5] That may be stretching rationality and control beyond the bounds of practicality. But we can identify four general types of nuclear exchanges: *reprisal*—a nuclear strike on a single or small number of cities in response to a similar attack on America or in response to a possibility of quickly ending a major conventional war; *counter-force attack*—a nuclear attack on an opposing nation's military forces but not on its population or industrial centers, the object being to disable or destroy the war-making forces and limit the destructive social consequences of the war; *slow-motion central attacks*—restrained but deliberately calculated and increasingly intensified attacks on central value targets like population and industrial centers, the object being to hurt the opposing nation enough that it will cease hostilities before the war reaches uncontrolled levels of intensity that destroy both or all nations; *spasm war*—all-out extermination attacks.

Nuclear weapons have been used only once. They were used in a reprisal attack on two Japanese cities. That was a brutal action, but it brought about a swift capitulation and eliminated the need for a large-scale land invasion of Japan. But Japan had no allies armed with nuclear weapons which would be used against America. In the Korean War and Vietnam War that situation did not exist, and so a nuclear reprisal strategy did not appear strategically safe no matter how strategically effective it might have been in the local conflicts.

The counter-force attacks appear to be a "sanitized" way to use nuclear weapons. That is, they would only be directed toward military forces, not population targets, and they could be carried out with small-scale nuclear weapons rather than the enormously destructive weapons on intercontinental missiles. But this strategy raises two unanswerable questions: Could the attacks be kept "clean" and not cause extensive civilian destruction? And could the war remain that limited once it had started?

The slow-motion central strategy requires cold-blooded nuclear attacks on civilian populations and would entail enormous social destruction. Such attacks border on the absurd. The warring nations and perhaps the world in general would be radically different at the war's end. Even though "victory" might be proclaimed by one side after the war, would it have any meaning, any worth for the survivors? Would the survivors envy the dead? Would surrender and occupation have been preferable? What if the strategy were successful in ending hostilities before the point of absurdity was reached? And how does one know where that point is and when it is reached?

These are questions without answers, involving situations never before experienced. One approach to resolving them is simply to banish them from the realm of moral acceptability. The enormity of destruction in time and space from even a reprisal strategy, especially when coupled with the danger of escalation, lead many people to see no redeeming justification for the use of nuclear weapons. The threshold between conventional and nuclear weapons should be made permanent and never crossed. The only way to retain any meaning at all for a morality of love and compassion is to keep it apart from nuclear warfare.

An alternate approach to that morality of purity is a morality of responsibility. This approach seeks to apply moral standards and choices to the dreadful issues forced on Christians by the facts of social life in this fallen world.

Is there room for moral choice in issues such as those of nuclear war? I believe so for several reasons. For one, while nuclear war raises some new and unique aspects to warfare, it does not raise issues that are different in kind from those of conventional warfare. Nuclear war raises the possibility of annihilating an enemy. But that possibility has always existed from earliest times and has been repeatedly carried out on defeated opponents. Capitulation in the face of nuclear war does not simply prevent nuclear war. It has consequences of its own which are pregnant with lethal danger.

Second, nuclear war does permit moral choice. A reprisal attack might leave five million dead but the war ended, while its rejection in favor of a large-scale land invasion might leave twenty million dead.

Third, Christians following a morality of responsibility believe their involvement in decisions can affect the moral quality of decisions, decisions both on the design of nuclear forces and the strategy and restraint adopted in their possible use.

Limited War

The danger of large-scale conventional war becoming nuclear and suicidal has sharply restrained political leaders from going to war in the last three decades. But the nature of international politics, the stakes involved in world affairs, and the dreams and goals of leaders have not changed.

In the late 1950s and early 1960s the process of decolonization was not free from turbulence. Some of the newly emerged nations were extremely frail and susceptible to outside pressures, and American leaders feared that Russia would try either to recolonize some of these nations in the name of "people's democracy" or try to subvert U.S. allies in these regions. But how could they be stopped?

American military policy in the 1950s was called "massive retaliation." This policy announced that America would respond at times and places and with methods of its own choosing to any effort of communist countries to expand their power. The clear implication was that we would defend the nations of the world by attacking Moscow with our nuclear forces. But by the end of that decade, political turbulence and subversion were being carried on in these new nations at a very low but lethal level. America was then faced with the choice of surrendering these areas or committing nuclear suicide for their sakes. Being an incredible policy, American leaders moved toward what they hoped would be a better one.

This new strategy, limited war, is distinguished by the clear restraint placed on goals, weapons, targets and geographic area. The intention is to deny any gains to an aggressor by matching his type of war and frustrating him. It is not designed to win a military victory or lead to the unconditional surrender of the opponent but to demonstrate that he could not achieve his goals and that further war was useless. It is also designed to prevent a *fait accompli*, whereby a nation suddenly strikes another nation and so presents America with an accomplished fact, putting great pressure on American leaders to do nothing rather than commit nuclear suicide. And third, limited war is a strategy designed to reduce the inhumanity and tragedy, and the political, economic and social destruction and dislocation of the war.

A limited war is to be more rational and controlled than previous wars and so less destructive. Restricting the goals of the war would prevent them from being absolutized, thereby justifying unrestricted warfare. It would also help keep the intensity of combat dampened, holding back the pressures to enlarge the intense fighting and costs.

What all of this means is that with the nature of international politics unchanged but with conventional war too deadly, any future World War would be a limited war. Limited wars would be fought for the same stakes as conventional war but by less destructive methods. If the Communists or anyone else were to try to take over the world, they would do it through subversion and small attacks in the non-West to win control of that part of the world and use it to strangle Europe rather than through large-scale war as in World Wars 1 and 2. The strategy of limited war was adopted by American leaders to stop that.

It sounded good, but it didn't work out in Vietnam because there are some crucial weaknesses in the doctrine. The strategy of limited war involves a shift in philosophy from using war for crushing and destroying an enemy to hurting and punishing him. But there are several dangers in this shift.

One is the tendency to fall into military deadlock at ever increasing levels of violence rather than in a decisive win or loss. For example, Robert McNamara, in a memo to President Johnson recommending a substantial increase in troop strength in Vietnam, stated:

> We should be aware that deployments of the kind I have recommended will not guarantee success. U.S. killed-in-action can be expected to reach 1,000 a month, and the odds are even that we will be faced in early 1967 with a "no-decision" at an even higher level.[7]

The Americans were not fighting to crush North Vietnam and occupy it. They were fighting only to make the North stop sending its troops into South Vietnam and pull out the troops already there. But the North Vietnamese did not accept the logic of this strategy as the North Koreans had once done. The Vietnamese kept fighting and matching our increases in the use of force. This brought back General Douglas MacArthur's statement that "there is no substitute for victory." But what is a victory today against a nation allied to two other nuclear powers?

The second weakness of the doctrine is the assumption that the opponent will remain committed to fighting a limited war. North Vietnam did not recognize and conform to our definition of the restraints and used sanctuary areas like Laos and Cambodia for its forces.

The third weakness of the limited war strategy is focused by Mao Tse-tung's doctrine of guerrilla war which he developed in his struggle against the Japanese occupation of China in the 1930s. Mao believed that if he could pull the Japanese forces into the interior of China, he could stretch their supply lines, use guerrilla forces for small sneak attacks rather than pitched battles, and use the people for assistance in information and protection. Japan would then be faced with a prolonged war with no decisive results the costs of which would cripple the Japanese industrial economy and break the will of the Japanese people to support the war. To a large extent that is what happened to the U.S. effort in Vietnam. Large industrial democracies cannot fight a long and indecisive war, and that weakness is crucial to the effectiveness of a limited war strategy.

Yet what is the alternative? Abandonment of large areas of the globe to aggressors? Growing authoritarianism by the American government to prevent the breaking of the economy and the will of the people? Reliance on nuclear threats to defend small nations? Reliance on large-scale conventional war and destruction, and hope it doesn't escalate or spill over into involvement with a nuclear ally of our opponent? The only answer can be to use a combination of military, economic and diplomatic incentives and punishments that is the least dangerous and destructive yet also effective. In other words, there is no clear answer, only trials with high dangers for errors.

Questions and Answers
Q. I don't see how you can justify the use of force. The

New Testament and the love ethic of Jesus clearly prohibit it. You sound like a theologian of the Pentagon.

A. Let me answer that in two parts. First, the use of military force is not an issue like extra-marital sex or the use of heroin. Issues like the last two involve a small circle of persons and possibly only one's self. On issues like those one can retain purity without causing enormous and widespread destruction and dislocation to thousands of other people. The use of military force is not an issue like that. Major consequences follow not only from its use but also its non-use. The rejection of force can have consequences just as lethal as force itself and not just for you but for thousands of your fellow citizens. A pure morality can be applied to issues confined to one's own life. But if you partake of the social life of a nation, then an ethic of responsibility must be adopted for those issues affecting the entire nation. A literal and absolutist application of the love ethic of Jesus cannot be made to issues of international politics.

Beyond that, the love ethic of Jesus does not abolish the Old Testament. The teachings of Jesus are interlaced with both the activities and the symbols of Israel in the Old Testament. A theology and morality of government and foreign policy cannot discount either the New or Old Testament and be built on one alone.

Q. Then you would accept nuclear war?

A. I don't want to hedge, but I can't give a blanket answer to that. Give me some examples.

Q. Well, the very fact that you refuse a blanket rejection is one answer in itself. But would you have advocated the use of nuclear weapons in Vietnam?

A. No, I wouldn't. Their use in that situation would not have been safe since North Vietnam had nuclear armed allies who could have launched nuclear reprisals on Japan or Europe, if not on America itself. Nor would it have been effective since we did not intend to subjugate North Vietnam.

Q. Would you have used them against Japan in World War 2?

A. Yes, I would have, though I would have preferred a "demonstration strike" in some unpopulated area first to try to convince the Japanese of what could happen to them.

Q. Would you engage in what you call "slow-motion central attacks"?

A. Well, before we leave the limited reprisal and counter-force strikes, let me make one other comment. If nuclear weapons continue to spread to other nations, especially the weak and disgruntled nations, the world will become so tense and dangerous that alliances will break. Commitments will be too dangerous to keep. In that case, America will have to be prepared to respond in kind or to accept continual and increasingly injurious demands backed by nuclear blackmail.

As to slow-motion attacks, I don't see that occurring under any conditions except between America and Russia. If the stake is American capitulation and the threat of a dismembered and degenerate peace, then I would. If the stake were simply an American capitulation to a Russian conventional occupation of Europe, then I would be very hesitant about going very far with such a strategy.

Q. How can moral standards possibly be applied in a war in the midst of dangers and unchristian commanders?

A. It is not easy, but considering war as just "doing a job" seems to be dangerous because that assumes there are no moral conflicts and because it reduces persons on both sides to mere cannon fodder.

Now, how can the standards of a Christian be applied? First of all, the Christian soldier must possess and maintain a developed sense of right and wrong. This sense comes from the leadership of the Holy Spirit which lives within to lead us in understanding and to motivate our will to do right. Thus we can be provided with guidance for all specific situations and, in general, we can escape or limit the "psychic numbing" of war—the loss of capacity to feel for others, which leads to a general brutalization of rationality and conscience.

Second, the Christian must be willing to restrain himself in situations, to refrain from doing anything the Spirit identifies as out of bounds for a Christian.

Third, God gives grace and forgiveness to the repentant. The Christian may become carried away under the pressures of fighting or be overcome with revenge when comrades are killed. He may feel guilty because he survived the war and many buddies did not. To the Christian God gives love and acceptance. The gross pressures of war cannot separate us from the love of God, so we can live and act and find meaning and grace in the acute moral dilemmas of war.

Finally, the Christian must not lose perspective on his place in time, humanity and affairs of state. Opponents must not be stripped of humanity, first because God loves them and second, because the ability to do so might be carried over into domestic life later. Additionally, wars do not last forever and affairs of state are not ultimate, so both of them must be subordinated to Christian perspective and judgment.

Q. Aren't you arguing that the Pentagon is immoral?

A. No. I am arguing that the Pentagon and its policies, like everything else in the life of a Christian, must not become ultimate or separated from moral standards. The Pentagon is an inescapable necessity for defense in this world. I am asking no more than to have the individual Christian apply rationality and moral standards to its policies.

Q. How can one consider it right to criticize the Defense Department when it is facing dedicated and powerful enemies overseas?

A. I do not believe the Defense Department should be attacked. The Department has a major and inescapable job in protecting this country. On the other hand, being run by mere men, its policies are not automatically the best; they may not be the most rational, the most effective or the most moral. They may even provoke danger rather than solely guard against danger. In such cases, I believe the Christian can and should have a role to play in democratic America in making those policies better.

Q. Did you imply that an engineer or secretary who works for a corporation involved even indirectly in weapons production is somehow immoral?

A. No. My point was that weapons production is widespread throughout our economy, which can have the effect of providing a justification for maintaining if not increasing the production of arms. Also, in the event that a Christian considers a particular weapon system to be immoral, he might consider himself to be in a moral dilemma if he worked at a corporation involved in the production of that weapon. Merely working for a defense industry is not immoral because weapons themselves and the Pentagon itself are not inherently immoral.

Q. If the military and political leaders and experts disagree, who am I to get involved?

A. Many of the military issues are extremely technical, and there must be a great deal of trust in the government to allow the assumption that whatever the government decides is good and just. But the very fact that disagreement within the government does exist means the Christian is not out of place if he disagrees with a specific proposal or policy. And the fact that positions of leaders may be based on their own parochial self-interest, like Admiral King's statement, and are never justified as self-interest but as being in the national interest, seems to me to imply that Christians should not be content with accepting the public statements of these leaders. The Christian, like every American, has an obligation to consider and evaluate the policies on his own. And then, as I shall explain in chapter seven, he can use the democratic process to effect a change.

Q. You said that the United States built the atomic

bomb because Nazi Germany was building one and im-
plied it was therefore justified in doing so. But it was
America that dropped the bomb on Japan. And I'm sure
Germany was building one because America was building
one. Why was the United States more justified than
Germany?

A. Leonardo da Vinci conceived of the submarine and
of its military potential. Such a weapon would have made
Venice the supreme military power in that age and would
have brought great honor to Leonardo. But he refused to
divulge his idea, fearing the results of one nation having
such a decisive military weapon. And so the submarine
was not built and used in war for another 400 years. That
was a great decision of Leonardo.

Making the same sort of decision would not have mat-
tered today, for all major nations heavily subsidize scientists and research so that it is common for similar discoveries to be made at the same time in different countries.
So America's refusal to build atomic weapons would not
have prevented the emergence of the atomic age.

Now, I would not argue that the United States was justified in dropping its first bomb on a population center. It
is tragically ironic that the bomb was dropped on the largest Christian population in Japan. I think that was a tragic
mistake.

But I still would have used an atomic weapon against
Japan if, after a demonstration strike, the war did not end
and a large-scale invasion was necessary to end the war. I
do not believe the United States, because it built the bomb,
can be compared to Nazi Germany. The use of atomic
weapons does not typify American strategy (they were not
used in Korea or Vietnam) as genocide did typify Nazi
society.

Q. But isn't science a danger? Isn't the progress of science in weapons, or even computers and mass production
techniques, dehumanizing people and turning them into
numbers?

A. No, I don't think so. The concentration camps and crematoriums of Nazi Germany were built because of the political leaders, not because of the scientists. Jacob Bronowski, in his book *The Ascent of Man*, makes an eloquent and moving plea that we see the dangers of dehumanizing people in the arrogance and the narrow self-righteousness of national leaders. The discoveries of science are here. We must now be attentive to who uses those discoveries and why. We must insure that our leaders be men of mental balance and that a witness and commitment to people be manifest in policy and action.

Basic Readings

Aron, Raymond. *The Great Debate*. New York: Doubleday. 1965. This book is a fine introduction to the theory of nuclear strategy that developed in this country in the late 1950s and especially in the early 1960s under the sponsorship of Secretary of Defense McNamara. It also explores the debate between the American nuclear strategists and those of Europe, particularly in France.

Brodie, Bernard. *Strategy in the Missile Age*. Princeton: Princeton University Press. 1959.

Halperin, Morton. *Defense Strategies for the Seventies*. Boston: Little-Brown Co. 1971. Halperin was Assistant Secretary of Defense under President Johnson, and a member of Henry Kissinger's White House staff. This is an informative and brief introduction to military strategy in different geographical regions of the world.

Kahn, Herman. *On Thermonuclear War*. Princeton: Princeton University Press. 1961. This is a massive and complete introduction to nuclear war. It has become a classic study, as well as the pre-eminent target of attack for opponents to nuclear strategy.

U.S. Secretary of Defense. *Annual Defense Department Report*. Washington, D.C.: Government Printing Office. These are annual reports and budget requests to Congress by the incumbent Secretary of Defense. They can be obtained free of charge from the Office of the Secretary of Defense. These could be supplemented by the annual report of the Chairman of the Joint Chiefs of Staff which can be obtained in the same manner.

U.S. Senate, Committee on Foreign Relations. *Nuclear Weapons and Foreign Policy*. Washington, D.C.: Government Printing Office. 1974.

———. *U.S.-U.S.S.R. Strategic Policies*. 1974.

———. *Briefing on Counterforce Attacks*. 1975.

Weigley, Russell F. *The American Way of War*. New York: Macmillan. 1973. This is a fine study of U.S. military history by a recognized authority.

V
DEMOCRACY
AND
POLICY

"You and the people with you will wear
yourselves out, for the thing is too heavy for you;
you are not able to perform it alone.... Choose
able men from all the people ... and place such men
over the people as rulers of thousands,
of hundreds, of fifties, and of tens.
And let them judge the people at all times ...
so it will be easier for you, and they will
bear the burden with you."
Exodus 18:18-22

Power is neither moral nor immoral, except in how and why it is used. Science and technological developments do not dehumanize people, except in how they are applied to people. The subjects of this chapter are the men and institutions that make those decisions which determine the morality or immorality in foreign policy.

What kinds of people are foreign policy leaders? To try to understand that we will look at politicians and bureaucrats. Who gets involved in making decisions? What is the role of public opinion in making foreign policy? Is there any legal or moral control over policy and activities? To explore these questions we will review Congress (the peoples' representatives), the State Department (the executive branch's leading department in foreign policy) and the Central Intelligence Agency (the institution that operates behind a cover of secrecy).

Politicians

Congressmen and presidents are politicians. They are not bureaucrats who are hired on the basis of merit, make a career by specializing in one subject and implement laws already in existence. Politicians, instead, are power-seekers and generalists whose careers are dependent upon being in the favor of the electorate.

Public office, the goal of politicians, is the center of authority. Those who hold public office hold the power to make decisions that affect the lives of other people. The major rewards of achieving public office are power and the status that goes with it.

Why do people seek power? The reasons are many, and different politicians will give different emphasis to the various reasons. Some seek political power to make changes they see as desirable in policy and society. They wish to serve the public, to build a better society, to implement their ideals and visions of justice. Others emphasize the personal rewards of public office. These people want recognition, glory and esteem to satisfy psychological needs. Political campaigning is an outlet for their personality, a means of becoming a center of attention, a focus of crowds, a subject of esteem. Self-interest in business is another reason some go into politics. Public office is a means of making important contacts, of expanding one's reputation. And some people enter politics for the pure pleasure of holding power over other people. Whether consciously or unconsciously, some people seek political power as an outlet for their assertive and domineering personalities.

Because there is no single explanation for why people seek power, there is no common bond that will lead them to see issues alike. And there is no reason to suppose that all politicians are driven by a subconscious lust for power (which some are) or by the hope to gain special business advantages over others (which some do).

The career backgrounds of politicians differ. Most are lawyers because that profession has distinct political advantages. Lawyers deal with public laws and policy, they have established wide contacts throughout their communities, and they have learned to persuade and move the emotions of people. But political offices are also held by persons from other occupations. There are teachers, salesmen, physicians, farmers, housewives and others. These different backgrounds also mean different perspectives, motives and goals.

The path to power is varied. Some politicians began in local political offices and worked their way up through county and state levels to national office. Others were recruited by local party clubs to run for a specific position. Other politicians started out by working as assistants to a congressman and then, being interested in politics but not wanting to be just an adviser any longer, resigned to return home and run themselves.

Despite all this variety, however, politicians have one problem in common: They can only get into office and stay in office by convincing a majority of voters in their areas to vote for them. Each political office has a specified term, after which the incumbents must stand for re-election. This electoral system has two magnificent consequences. Elections force the politicians to remain aware of the problems and opinions of their citizens. It insures some degree of governmental responsiveness to the needs of people as well as to those of society as a whole. The second consequence is that new people can become involved in politics. Each election opens the possibility that a person with newer ideas or a closer relationship with the people will be elected.

These consequences mean that foreign policy issues may be judged on the basis of domestic needs or campaign pragmatics rather than on the merits of the issues themselves. Also, continuity may be lost in policy if major political leaders in Congress who specialize in foreign policy are constantly changing.

What about political parties? Don't members of political parties vote according to the beliefs of their parties? No. There is no set of beliefs to which members of a party must adhere. The beliefs held by party members from different sections of the nation vary greatly. Parties have no important sources of power to force members to believe or vote a certain way. That is due to primary elections. The parties cannot determine who their candidate will be; the voters choose the party's candidate in primaries. A set pattern of beliefs cannot be enforced, and so the parties are not important vehicles for developing unity among politicians.

The Divided Congress

The American Congress is one of the world's few great institutions of representative democracy. Its members are freely elected and are actively involved in making national policy, both foreign and domestic. It represents a wide range of public opinion and acts as an independent branch of government, not as a rubber stamp.

But the Congress also symbolizes vast inefficiency. It is slow, ponderously slow. It has been controlled by southern conservatives until just the last few years. And it is an arena for enormous egos and ambitions.

The Founding Fathers of the American government were divided—should the Congress represent people or states? Consensus was gained when they agreed that it should represent both. And so today there are two houses of Congress, a Senate and a House of Representatives. Representatives have two-year terms to force them to constantly run for office and so stay close and responsive to public opinion. Senators, representing whole states, serve six years. They are therefore more insulated from changes in public opinion and theoretically will take a more national perspective on issues.

So disagreement and divergence of perspective are built

into the government by its very structure. Also, legislation must face a kind of "double jeopardy," passing debate, amendment, opposition and finally a majority vote in identical form in two houses of Congress.

If you go to Washington, D. C. and visit Capitol Hill, you will likely see only three or four senators in the Senate and six or seven representatives in the House. The reason is that the bulk of the work of Congress is done in committees. It would be impossible to formulate or analyze national policy changes with a group of 100 senators of 435 representatives. So, to speed up the process and to provide concentrated analysis on legislation, the members of Congress are assigned to committees.

Each committee has a specific area of responsibility and uses subcommittees to investigate and study particular topics in that area. Thus, each house has a committee on foreign relations, with subcommittees for selected topics within that area. But even that committee does not cover every aspect of foreign policy. Military affairs are the domain of the committees on armed services. Economic affairs, space policy, atomic energy activities and other topics go to other committees.

These committees, and particularly their chairmen, carry enormous influence in Congress regarding their topics. They have listened to expert witnesses, studied the legislation, modified it, argued about it and voted on it. So by the time legislation reaches the floor of each house, the Congress as a whole is usually disposed to accept the recommendations of the committees.

The committees are organized along partisan lines. The majority party in Congress has the right to have more members on each committee than does the minority party. And the majority party selects the chairmen. Thus, when the president's party does not control Congress, the committees' work and witnesses and recommendations can be organized against the president. The criterion for selecting chairmen is seniority. The committee member from the majority party that has the longest record of service on the committee becomes the chairman. This is to ensure that the chairman has the most knowledge about the issues that come before the committee. But at times it has been a "senility" system rather than a seniority system, for chairmen are well advanced in years and well entrenched in attitudes.

The responsibilities of Congress are numerous. The Constitution authorizes Congress to declare war, provide for the military forces, regulate foreign trade, and give advice and consent on the appointment of ambassadors and top level officials in departments and agencies.

There are also other unspecified but important responsibilities. One of those is to educate the public. Congressmen who disagree with accepted policy can work to convince the public that some alternate policy is better. This education function is accomplished through committee hearings that are reported by the media, by speeches given in the Congress, and by speeches a congressman gives while traveling around to colleges and clubs.

Another responsibility is to oversee the execution of laws and policy. Are the adopted policies working? Have they been modified in practice? Are there abuses, arbitrary decisions or misjudgments that have negated or distorted the intended impact of the law? These are concerns of Congress, concerns that are carried out by investigating the executive branch and its operations.

Another responsibility is to represent public opinion. That is not easy. Have you ever told or written your views to a congressman or senator? If not, then how are they supposed to represent you? In the absence of widespread communication of views and opinions to their offices, congressmen either vote their own preferences or respond to organized public opinion. Groups which have special interests and stakes in matters of foreign policy organize themselves to lobby Congress. Thus, while Congress has the responsibility to represent public opinion, it is normally the opinion of organized groups, which may represent a very small segment of the public, that get represented.

A related responsibility is the protection of dissent. When an adviser or departmental officer disagrees with the policy of a president, the job of that adviser or official is jeopardized. The president is free to fire officials in his administration. But he cannot fire a congressman. All he can do is not invite him to White House dinners or to his children's weddings or for a trip in Air Force One. Dissent is protected in Congress. That dissent may or may not be correct. But the government cannot be purged by a president to stifle opposition.

Frustration

Congressional involvement in matters of foreign policy is not always easy or beneficial. The proper role for Congress is the subject of debate in the government, the academic community and the public at large.

The president and his officials are protective of their prerogatives in foreign policy. Presidents and their advisers want flexibility in policy and unity in the government when they are negotiating with foreign powers. Those desires have led to widespread use of secrecy and a restriction on the number of people involved in policy-making. In either case, congressmen are usually those left out. And if a congressman or congressional committee pushes too hard for information about an area the president feels is sensitive, distorted or totally false information may be given. One recent example was the claim by State Department officials, in response to questions by a congressional committee, that America was not involved in the 1973 military overthrow of the government of Chile. Later they had to admit to that same committee that America was indeed involved.

Another area of frustration is the lack of effective impact on policy. New congressmen find their initiatives and recommendations either ignored or totally blocked by the entrenched power of the eldest leaders. All congressmen find their time filled with multiple duties to various committees, constituents, visitors, meetings and discussions, and to studying and pushing their own recommendations. The range of topics is also immense. A congressman wishing to specialize in foreign policy may find his time devoured by congressional concern with health insurance, energy policy, economic growth and a host of other highly important and complicated topics. The amount of work is enormous and can, in time, lead to complacency or despair.

Most of the time the president and his officials develop and execute foreign policy. Opponents can only make speeches and nibble at the edges of that policy. But times do occur when the Congress unifies itself and makes decisions that affect policy. Sometimes that happens despite the pressure and pleas of the president. In recent years Congress has passed a War Powers Act that requires specific congressional approval within sixty days of a president's decision to use American military forces abroad. The Congress has prohibited further American military involvement in Vietnam, Cambodia and Angola. It cut off military aid to Turkey and launched a penetrating (and leaky) investigation of the Central Intelligence Agency.

These decisions may have been major mistakes or they may have been moments of great congressional wisdom. But in any case, two items should be noted. First, the Congress cannot make policy. By its size, structure and variety of opinions, it is much better suited to preventing the president's policy. Second, the long-range impact of such preventive actions is to set the limits of permissibility, the boundaries of what is acceptable policy.

The Organization Men
The bureaucracy of the United States, like the government in general, is designed to prevent the rise of a dictator. It is decentralized and nonpartisan. Even though the bureaucracy is huge, its division and decentralization hin-

ders tyranny. Many large and small departments, nearly all of them independent of each other, have foreign affairs responsibilities. Instead of a single Department of Foreign Affairs, there is a Department of State, a Department of Defense, an Agency for International Development, an Arms Control and Disarmament Agency, a Central Intelligence Agency, and an Information Agency. Additionally, domestic-oriented departments like Agriculture, Labor, Commerce and Treasury have foreign responsibilities and their own foreign affairs staffs. In such a setting, no one person or group is in full control.

The independence of departments and their specialized functions generate the development of certain organizational stakes for each department. One of these is the protection and promotion each department gives its own special role in foreign relations. Employees of the Agency for International Development are prone to exaggerate the power of foreign aid in world affairs just as military men in the Department of Defense are prone to exaggerate the effectiveness of military power. This leads officials to press for significant roles for their departments in all U.S. activities. They also tend to view any attempt to restrict or modify their activities as a threat and any attempt by an outsider to direct the department's activity in another country as meddling or unauthorized interference. A top State Department official told Congress:

I have had other agencies say this to me: 'Our program abroad is our program, we have had it established by Congress and, therefore, it isn't any of your business trying to tell us whether or not we need more people and whether or not we should be doing certain things abroad; this is our program.'[1]

A second organizational stake is employee loyalty. Agencies want to maximize their employees' contributions and to retain their best people. What they do is convince employees of the importance of the department's work, convincing them that they are working for an impor-

tant cause. But the danger is that this loyalty will be parochial, directed toward the agency at the expense of the
overall government effort.

All of this stifles the ability of anyone to capture control
of the government. It also represents each specialty in foreign affairs so all points of view are considered and no divergent opinion is suppressed. But at the same time, the
ability of the United States to develop and operate a gov-
ernmentwide package of activities in a mutually reinforc-
ing way is severely limited. Agreements on responsibilities and the nature of programs must come through hundreds of interdepartmental committees where each department is equal and decisions are reached by consensus.
This process promotes compromising, bargaining, trade-
offs and ambiguity, thereby diluting the precision and
forcefulness of what the United States can do abroad.

The nonpartisan nature of the government is achieved
through the Civil Service System which requires that persons be hired and promoted on the basis of their abilities,
not their support for the president or his programs. This
preserves the objectivity of the officials and protects them
in disagreements, for they cannot be fired or otherwise dis-
missed for disagreement. But it further concentrates their
loyalties around their departments. For it is the department that hires them, pays and promotes them, and provides their retirement system. The noncareer officials, the
heads of the departments and their bureaus, are appointed
by the president, but they are relatively short-term when
measured against the twenty-five or thirty-five years service of a career official. And those department heads are
normally lawyers or businessmen with no experience in
foreign affairs who must rely on the briefings and analysis
by their staffs.

As organizational stakes can impinge on one's evaluation of a proposed policy or activity so can personal stakes.
Most bureaucrats have personal goals of their own like
promotions, pay increases, prestige and power. Some-

times the fate and effectiveness of a certain policy or operation can decisively affect the reputation and so the goals of a bureaucrat.

On the basis of the differences and relative intensity of motivation which these organizational and personal stakes generate, we can identify four different types of bureaucrats. *Climbers* are persons intensely motivated by considerations of power, income and prestige. They will evaluate each policy and action by its potential impact on their advancement. *Preservers* are persons who have reached a satisfactory level of income and status and now wish only to evade important decisions so they will not make major mistakes and be demoted. *Zealots* are intensely committed to a department or policy and will freely expend their energy and reputation to defend and advance it. *Statesmen* are bureaucrats whose loyalty runs first to America as a whole and its welfare. They will disregard organizational and personal considerations in evaluating policies and operations.

This setting with its organizational stakes and these persons with their personal stakes are important factors in generating conflict and disagreement within the bureaucracy. This precludes any undemocratic or conspiratorial group from capturing control. But, on the other hand, policy is diluted, policy development and decision-making advance at a crawl and different policies can be pursued in the same country by different departments. The problem is not that officials are slow or dull but that the structural arrangements in which they must work institutionalize deadlock or compromise. Thus, an ambassador can be kept waiting for days or weeks for a policy response to be formulated toward some development in his country. Also as changed conditions are only slowly recognized, a greater time lag can develop. Officials grow accustomed to routine and well-established policy. Developing a new policy can be an agonizing process.

For this reason a president is tempted to make all policy

in the White House with his own private staff. This speeds up policy development and saves it from interdepartmental dilution. But it also runs the risk of missing crucial ingredients available from experienced officials. It also generates high levels of insecurity and suspicion in the career bureaucracy.

In 1971, for example, a kind of bureaucratic espionage occurred when President Nixon and Henry Kissinger were secretly planning Kissinger's trip to China. The anxiety over what was being secretly planned without the advice and consent of the military was so great that secret memos and study papers were stolen from Kissinger's briefcase by military officers in the White House. Those papers were then copied and sent to the Joint Chiefs of Staff.

The Bowl of Jelly

The State Department is the official and central institution for conducting American foreign relations. It formulates policy proposals, makes decisions on specific daily matters, reports and interprets the activities and trends around the world, and speaks for the president in other countries. It carries on negotiations with other regimes and is responsible for overseeing and integrating the overseas activities of other government departments.

That is a huge task, and the State Department has not done it well. President Kennedy, in a moment of exasperation, referred to it as "a bowl of jelly,"[2] an agency that was slow, ponderous and unwilling to assert leadership. But there are reasons for this. The Department has been hampered in fulfilling its central role because its power has been lost to White House staffers, to a suspicious and critical Congress, to reluctant colleagues in other departments, and to its own ponderous structure, personnel and operating style.

The major portion of the Department's activities are carried out through five regional bureaus representing major regions of the world. The bureaus are headed by

Assistant Secretaries of State who are appointed by the president and who are responsible to him for implementing his policies in their specific regions. Below the Assistant Secretaries are Country Directors. They coordinate activities, relay communications between the Department and the Embassy, make decisions, advise superiors and other departments, draft messages, and obtain the agreement of other involved bureaus on directives sent to the Embassy.

Each regional bureau has its own perspectives and traditions. These determine its approach to specific countries, its attitudes toward other departments' activities in the region, its assumptions concerning the importance of the region to U.S. purposes in the world and its evaluations of danger to that region or from that region. These perspectives develop over time and harden under opposition from other bureaus, departments and other nations within and outside the region.

For example, the Far East Bureau was purged and chastised by Congress for the supposed "loss" of China. It has been staffed by "hard-line" Cold Warriors ever since. The Latin American Bureau developed very close and favorable relations with the countries in that region. The acknowledged premier regional bureau is the European, which is heavily pro-English. The involvement of England with former colonies in Africa, Asia and Latin America makes this bureau a frequent participant in policy development and decisions in other regional bureaus.

These different perspectives and interlocking interests have caused deep conflicts between bureaus and other departments, and between career men and political appointees. A recent ambassador in Africa recently told Congress:

> Despite the cascade of colonial authority in the last two decades, our allies have deep sentimental, financial, and military ties with their former colonies.... In the Department of State, policy is often thrashed out in a logrolling contest between the "European desks" and

the new offices dealing with the new countries. This is understandable, but it is unfortunately true that policy may sometimes be subject to a kind of immobilism or an imprecision in definition caused by these conflicts of views.[3]

Other bureaus organized around a function or nonregional topic like international organizations, economic affairs or political-military affairs also exist within the Department. They impinge upon policy-making in the geographical regional bureaus too.

The personnel of the Department are in a stage of transition. The Foreign Service has traditionally considered itself an elite club which alone understood the foreign world. It alone had the required characteristics of perception, sound judgment, panoramic understanding and intuition tempered by the fires of experience. This attitude, and their perception of their job as personal goodwill ambassadors who work by going to parties and mingling with the social and political elite of their host country, earned diplomats the name and reputation of "cookie-pushers."

This elitist image was reinforced by a recruitment policy that emphasized select ivy league schools and a promotion system that generated strong pressures for uniformity of views. Each year all Foreign Service Officers were evaluated in "efficiency reports" and a certain number "selected out." The report, long and detailed, including both a check list of qualities and essays, was highly vulnerable to subjective attitudes. Each person had to insure his promotion by always pleasing his superior and never calling his activities into question. The "selection out" procedure was recently declared unconstitutional and replaced with a procedure more open to participation by all concerned.

The "foreign service mind" was also developed through rotation of assignments. The generalist, not the expert in a particular subject, was considered the ideal diplomat because broad perspective and experience in dealing with all sorts of people under stress situations were desired. But officers were not in assignments long enough to effect any sizable change (and change would reflect upon superiors anyway). When a crisis developed, persons with some depth of understanding of the issues would be unavailable, having been transferred to another part of the world.

Frustration at not being able to come to grips with real problems was increased by watching choice ambassadorial positions—the culmination of the career ladder—used by presidents as rewards for political favorites. Career Foreign Service Officers saw themselves superceded by men who were amateurs. They had no acquaintance in foreign affairs or with the specific country, its language and traditions. Their business careers and standards of living made it next to impossible to sympathize with or even begin to understand the peoples in the nations of Asia, Africa and Latin America. Some of these ambassadors turned out to be quite good, others so bad they were declared persona non grata and told to leave the country.

The small size of the Department, the enormous number of developments occurring simultaneously around the world, and the ideal of the personalistic diplomatic elite all led to downgrading planning and relying on the intuition and experience of diplomats to respond when crises arose. But this "brush fire" approach to crisis decision-making has come under mounting criticism.

Many officials within and outside the Department are pressing for a new reliance on management and in-depth expertise. A series of planning and management systems have been introduced and discarded in a search for a method to bring the kind of certainty and control to the State Department that McNamara brought to the Defense Department. But this new approach, a reaction to the "cookie-pusher" style of diplomacy, may be a misreading of the nature of diplomacy and negotiation.

Diplomacy

Diplomacy is the process whereby two or more independent nations attempt to reach agreement on a subject. That process may be simple or it may be unbelievably long and frustrating. The result may be a mutually beneficial agreement or no agreement at all.

Friendly nations are normally conscious of each other's interests and problems. Diplomatic discussions usually take place within the framework of widely shared values and objectives. Here, compromise and mutual concessions are relatively easy and produce a workable agreement. But still, even in a friendly atmosphere, independent and sovereign nations always have different interests, needs and priorities and so will demand mutual concessions. No nation will give in completely to another; no nation will get everything it wants.

Among competing nations there are few common values that will support agreements requiring trust and good faith for their observance. Even if both sides want an agreement, they may be too suspicious of each other's motives and values to get it. Each can feel that if it initiated a compromise or concession, that action would be perceived as weakness and lead the other nation to stiffen its demands.

It is also possible in either case that one party in the negotiations simply does not want an agreement on the issue. It may want, instead, a propaganda platform or the world image of a peace-lover or a camouflage for its real purposes. In that case, the other party may resort to rather clear inducements by offering rewards or threatening punishment of some sort. It may promise a large foreign aid package, technical information or public support in a dispute with another nation. It may mobilize its armed forces, cut off trade and tourism, or give military support to the other nation's enemy. These sorts of inducements reflect the fact that nations do not operate on reason or the common good alone. They operate on what is good for them.

Can it ever be in the interest of the United States to make

agreements with adversaries like Russia and China? What guarantees do we have that they will keep their word? Are we not simply deluding ourselves to believe that we can do business with these kinds of nations?

The answer relates back to the fact that nations do what is seen as good for themselves. Any agreement that can be worked out in a way that is good for them as well as good for us will be accepted and observed. The key is to create conditions of power that make the agreement desirable to the other nations or to link the agreement to some power arrangement that will make it desirable.

The Strategic Arms Limitation Agreements between the United States and Russia are examples. Russia began building an antiballistic missile system. We asked them to agree with us not to build such a system and they refused. So Congress passed an authorization for the United States to build its own ABM system, and we began to do so. Then we went back to the Russian leaders and pointed out to them that the value of their system would be negated by ours, and they would have spent billions of dollars and have nothing effective in the end. Under those circumstances, an agreement to limit the building of such systems was adopted. The threat to build our own was a decisive bargaining chip.

Another example is the Kissinger negotiations in the Middle East in 1974. The United States had used its pressure to stop the 1973 war before any decisive victor emerged. That left a political-military situation in which both the Arabs and Israelis were unconquered and hence equal. With the war stopped and arsenals resupplied, neither side really wanted the war to begin again. When the United States coupled that desire with a pledge of massive foreign aid, Kissinger was able to get each side to begin negotiations and to grant mutual concessions that resulted in a cease-fire and a demilitarized zone and in 1975 a partial Israeli pullback.

In short, diplomacy is a form of political competition

and struggle. The results of negotiations depend in part on factors of power and self-interest. But diplomacy is also psychological. The cynical view that a diplomat is a man sent abroad to lie for his country cannot be maintained in the real world. Diplomacy at the very least requires the assumption that one can believe the statements of other diplomats.

Diplomacy also requires the ability to overcome hostile and suspicious images and attitudes in other nations. Nations and their leaders have mental images, stereotyped beliefs, set reasoning patterns, emotional tilts toward friendliness or hostility, and dispositions to trust or suspect other nations and leaders. Working with such psychological attitudes—dispelling the unfavorable and promoting the favorable—is why a major role of diplomats is pushing cookies. And that is why diplomats must be more than just managers of aid, information and cultural exchange programs. Diplomatic relations are political and psychological, and when a situation arises in which rewards or threats are inappropriate or ineffective in removing hostile attitudes, the patient, personal work of an ambassador might.

Diplomacy also has elements of vision and style. American foreign policy has been limited by the tendency of American leaders, trained in law or business, to see diplomacy as crisis management, devising winning responses to individual crises as they arise. Adversaries, on the other hand, have pursued foreign policy like chess players combining a series of events (or crises) into a harmonious strategy aimed at a predefined goal. American leaders have tended to view each strategic confrontation as unique. Successful diplomacy means amassing a long series of profitable "wins."

But that approach destroys all semblance of priorities among crises, exaggerates a "loss," and makes U.S. foreign policy nothing more than a series of ad hoc defensive responses to whatever moves our adversaries might initiate.

American leaders correctly recognized as a delusion the belief that only one nation can move history and world events as it wishes. So they did not devise some world strategy like Hitler laid out in *Mein Kampf*. But in their purely defensive posture they wasted opportunities.

What an adequate diplomat must have is an intuitive, inspired vision of the world, including an understanding of the world conditions that are favorable for his nation, a recognition of the historic relationships and relative importance between events, and a vision of the conditions that will support peace, stability and cooperation.

The diplomat is the person in history that promotes reconciliation and agreements among peoples and nations —moving the inert, deflecting the hostile, disintoxicating hatred, perceiving and explaining the common good, seeing and defending the essential. He is the Statesman, rather than the Conqueror or the Visionary described in the second chapter. He makes use of the military's power and the people's aspirations, combining them into an appropriate condition of security and legitimacy. He weaves together reality and vision into a workable and desirable web of the possible and the desirable. This makes the diplomat a central figure in creating conditions of just and lasting peace. Henry Kissinger, for example, trained in politics, not law or business, has demonstrated in the Middle East and China the potentials of a diplomat's ability to bring peace, reconciliation and cooperation to peoples divided by bitter chasms of hatred, suspicion and violence.

The Christian must recognize that the diplomat is limited since he works with other sovereign nations and must contend with their power. This means he has to compromise, and compromise can be attacked:

> What is defined as justice at home becomes the subject of negotiation abroad. It is thus no accident that many nations, including our own, view the international arena as a forum in which virtue is thwarted by the clever practice of foreigners.[4]

Compromise is a necessity. This reinforces the need for a sense of purpose and a sense of the essential and the desirable. The diplomat must recognize that the long-range cannot be lost in the pressures of the immediate. Personal compromise with evil in one's own life is intolerable. But compromise and flexibility among nations are required in this world of power struggles if cooperation and trust are going to be maintained.

The PICKLE Factory

Information, or intelligence, is a serious and, at times, critical factor in foreign policy. If information is distorted or incomplete, the attitudes of American leaders can be mistakenly hostile or mistakenly complacent. Their programs can be useless or insufficient. Information that is biased to promote one particular agency's influence or an individual's personal advancement can warp policy priorities or belittle the risks involved in a proposed action. Contradictory information can paralyze decision-making or make a new policy initiative self-defeating.

Diplomacy and security both require good information. The SALT Agreements would have been impossible if American leaders had not known specifically the numbers, types and caliber of Russian missiles. A vital element in the American peace efforts in the Middle East was knowledge of the military capabilities of the nations involved and how introducing new weapons from the outside would affect the balance of strength.

One source of information for the White House is the President's Intelligence Checklist, or PICKLE. This is a daily report from the Central Intelligence Agency about important world developments of the preceding day.

The Central Intelligence Agency was established to provide American leaders with the most complete and accurate information possible. It was to be a central agency for gathering, reviewing and interpreting the information from its own sources and those of other intelligence groups. The CIA was also set up under the authority of the National Security Council to advise on intelligence matters and to perform "other functions and duties" relating to national security. The agency was specifically denied police power, subpoena authority and internal security functions so it would not evolve into a secret police like Hitler's Gestapo.

The CIA is an independent agency not a staff of some other department. This was intended to reduce the chance of bias or distortion in its analysis. And while it is the central agency in intelligence, it is not the exclusive one. Intelligence staffs were retained in the military services, the State Department and elsewhere so no gaps in information would exist and so disagreement and divergent analysis would not be suppressed.

The ability of U.S. intelligence groups to gather information is phenomenal. A great deal can be obtained through public documents like foreign newspapers, by contacts with important leaders in other countries or by simple observation and analysis through American embassies.

Other information is gathered through photographic devices. The main photographic source is the observation satellite. The United States maintains a network of such satellites that provides visual coverage of selected countries. When a particular item is to be investigated a special satellite is orbited with a camera capable of spotting objects two feet wide from an altitude of one hundred miles. The photos are then ejected from the satellite in a special canister that will deploy a parachute to slow its fall and enable it to be recovered by a special aircraft. Another satellite system monitors missile firings and can warn of an attack.

Electronic information is another type of intelligence effort. This involves the use of ships (like the U.S.S. Pueblo) and submarines to monitor conversations between the military units of another nation, providing clues to codes and strategy. They also monitor radar capabilities and scanning zones in order to devise penetration routes. Mock raids are also run toward another nation, hoping to stimulate a defensive response to time and analyze that nation's response capabilities.

Intelligence agents also seek political and economic information. The health of a foreign leader, the domestic support or opposition to a foreign regime, the policy orientations of the top leaders and advisers in other nations, the viability of the economy and its future prospects—these and similar questions are important in planning policy and negotiating positions. Many times this information can be obtained quite openly from tourists, businessmen and embassy personnel. Some of it is obtained by undercover agents and eavesdropping devices like telephone taps. As late as 1971 the CIA was sending Laotian teams as far as two hundred miles into China.

Despite the centrality of the CIA, its studies and reports are not final. When the National Security Council requests a study, the CIA's Board of National Estimates divides the study into component parts and assigns them to appropriate intelligence units within and outside the CIA. The Board then collects the finished studies, assembles and coordinates them, and returns the result to the intelligence units for review and comments.

The revised report is then sent to the U.S. Intelligence Board, which comprises the chiefs of all intelligence units, chaired by the Director of the CIA. This board then reviews and revises it, and finally sends it to the National Security Council.

The final report, therefore, represents the analysis and interpretation of the entire intelligence establishment. This process of multiple sources and multiple revisions is designed to reduce and hopefully eliminate all bias, distortion and gaps in the knowledge available to American leaders. This is a time-consuming process. But PICKLE keeps the president informed of all important developments of the preceding day by sending him daily reports.

The Operations Division

In addition to these intelligence studies the CIA has carried out certain secret political activities. These actions, carried out through the Operations Division of the CIA, raise disturbing moral and political questions about the role of the CIA in American foreign policy.

These covert operations began mildly enough. They were designed to provide aid to democratic groups in Western Europe during the years Stalin was subsidizing communist organizations in those same countries. During the 1950s these operations evolved from simply supporting friends to subverting foes. The foe could be the actual government, as when the CIA aided the overthrow of the Arbenz Government of Guatemala in 1954. It could also be anti-government insurgents, as when the CIA aided in the suppression of insurgents in Peru in the mid-1960s.

These covert activities have been varied. The CIA has provided weapons, military training and military supplies to various governments and insurgent groups, including Burma and Indonesia. It owns its own airlines, like Air America, and runs a training school for foreign policy called International Police Services, Inc. The CIA has given money and other support to strengthen labor unions and democratic political parties in Finland in the 1950s, and to promote strikes and economic chaos, as in Chile in the early 1970s. Military services like providing ground control for the Laotian government's Air Force have come from the CIA. It has recruited, established and maintained political leaders in countries like Iran, Vietnam and the Congo. It has contaminated Cuban food supplies and plotted "executive action"—the assassination of foreign governmental leaders.[5]

An Invisible Government?

That last activity is probably the most ruthless of the covert activities, and poses serious and urgent questions about this agency. First of all, are these types of covert activities necessary? An adequate answer to that is hindered by the fact that not all such activities are known. It is also hindered by the inability to say with certainty what "would have happened" if they had not been carried out. But some conclusions can be drawn despite these limitations.

Such covert activities provide methods that can, in favorable circumstances, obstruct or replace a hostile regime, and do so without U.S. Marines and Army tanks. This assumes that the regime that is the target of U.S. covert action is actually dangerous to American security. It is recognized that while interference in another nation's internal affairs may cause diplomatic disturbances and discord, peace is not guaranteed by noninterference.

But the disturbing conclusion that emerges from analyzing the known and more serious covert actions is that the long-range impact seems negligible. Some seem almost counter-productive. In Chile, for example, the United States was indirectly involved in a military takeover of the government. The United States had refused aid to the increasingly socialistic government of President Allende. It had acted through the CIA to disrupt the Chilean economy in an effort to create so much domestic disorder that the Chilean military would take over. The military did act, overthrowing the government, killing President Allende and instituting a harsh and repressive rule by a clique of military generals.

A second question is how much these activities are endorsed by America's top policy-making leaders. Or, put another way, are the officials in charge of covert activities operating independently? Do they comprise an "invisible government" and actually run the foreign policy of the United States?

In answering that question one must realize that the CIA has distinct characteristics which could enable it to play a behind-the-scenes role in controlling foreign policy. It has undisclosed amounts of money. It has high caliber agents. It has the latest in technology and weaponry. Its agents remain in particular countries longer than do State Department officials so the CIA agents can develop closer relationships and greater influence with foreign leaders, political groups and cliques.

And the CIA has the blanket of secrecy. There are no press briefings on its activities. The charter that authorizes these covert activities was approved by the National Security Council not the Congress which established the CIA. And that charter is still secret. Secrecy pervades the CIA Headquarters itself. No names or titles appear on doors. Agents sharing the same office do not know what each other is working on.

This secrecy protects the covert operations. It also amplifies the reputation of the Agency for sinister designs and uncontrolled power. But this secrecy also means that the covert agents might operate without the benefit of their own agency's information and analysis.

In a very real sense there are two CIAs, the intelligence branch and the covert branch. The CIA Headquarters is shaped like a giant H with the intelligence branch on the right side and the covert operations located on the left. What has happened is that this covert branch has grown up as a second CIA, grown up alongside of, but apart from, the original CIA.

What kind of controls operate on this covert portion? There is a central leadership in the CIA with authority over both sides. President Kennedy sent a special secret letter to all U.S. ambassadors instructing them to coordinate any CIA operations in their country with established U.S. policy. President Kennedy also moved responsibility for any future military operations like the Bay of Pigs operation from the CIA to the Joint Chiefs of Staff in the Pentagon. The Armed Services Committees of Congress have authority to review CIA operations since the CIA budget is hidden in the Pentagon budget. Finally, there is a special White House committee that guides and reviews these covert activities.

There are, in short, definite mechanisms for control of CIA operations. So the question becomes whether or not the machinery is used, and how it is used. The congressional committees have used their authority very sparingly and superficially. That has led to calls by some congressmen for new watchdog committees. The presidential level committee has been used, and in fact has been the source for initiation of covert activities. But it, like the central leadership of the CIA, can know only what they are told by the CIA agents or discover from other sources. The commission President Ford established in 1975 to study the CIA portrayed it as an agency that was defective in internal control.

Is the CIA an invisible government? In the sense of being a secret agency that does carry out some policy, it is. In the sense of being an independent invisible government, it is not. And in the sense of being able to run foreign policy, it does not seem to be. But in the sense of being a secret tool through which the top American leaders can secretly pursue policies that are at variance with their publicly stated policies, it is an invisible government. That raises the specter of tremendous dangers.

An American Gestapo?

The CIA's unique combination of the highest caliber technology, money and secrecy gives it the potential for being a secret police, a Gestapo. If it were to operate outside the bounds of public law and operate against American citizens, it would be a threat to American democracy.

In its December 22, 1974 issue, *The New York Times* newspaper reported that the CIA was involved in a massive and illegal domestic intelligence operation and that that operation was directed against American citizens. The FBI is charged with internal or domestic investigation and the CIA is specifically prohibited by law from this. The significance of the newspaper report was that the CIA was, in fact, operating inside the U.S. against

U.S. citizens. And its methods, including wiretaps and burglaries, were illegal.

In response to the allegations President Ford established The Commission on CIA Activities within the United States. Its June 1975 Report confirmed the charges. The CIA had set up a special unit called Operation CHAOS. Files were built on 7,200 American citizens and 1,000 organizations. Its computer indexed 300,000 names, and its methods of gathering information included illegal means, including the opening of mail.[6]

Crisis in Policy; Democracy in Politics

The covert operations raise moral and political questions about the appropriateness of clandestine interference and subversion in other countries. The CHAOS operation raises problems associated with a secret agency in an open society, deliberate deception in a democracy.

The Christian as American citizen should have a number of concerns about the CIA. The first one concerns covert operations. There are demands that all covert activities cease and recommendations that covert activities be taken away from the CIA and located in some new agency. Demands for elimination of covert operations are premature. There may be times yet when undercover support of friendly forces or subversion of hostile forces may be of great advantage to the United States.

Rather than being eliminated altogether, covert activities should be reduced in number and more effective internal controls be placed on them. To stop a coup (the sudden overthrow of a government by a small group) in another country or to promote one may be important for U.S. foreign policy. But to have it planned and executed independently of the purposes and approval of the top government leadership is unacceptable. This may require new congressional watchdog committees or a new CIA structure. But to try to eliminate them entirely would simply drive them further underground. In 1974 Congress passed the Hughes Amendment that prohibits the use of CIA funds for covert operations in other countries unless the president specifically determines them to be important for national security and reports it to the House and Senate foreign relations committees. If that can be enforced it will be an important new control.

Again we have to recognize the principle of proportionality. We have to recognize that answers are not simple because unforeseen consequences flow from nonaction as well as action.

But the competition inherent in international politics cannot be invoked to justify every kind of action. Even the starkest kind of covert operation, executive action, remains nothing more than murder unless the conditions are so critical and dangerous that it becomes an act of war. A "cover story" is not just protection of secrecy, it is lying.

Another area of concern is the psychology and standards of acceptability that these activities produce. Extensive use of covert operations runs the danger of producing a segment of government agents accustomed to operating outside the confines of normal morality and law. They can erode the government's commitment to political restraint that has to pervade a society for a democracy to exist. The Christian citizen should be concerned that covert operations remain small in number and tightly controlled. They should also be scrupulously reviewed by both the White House and Congress to be sure such activities are not being used in the service of domestic partisan purposes.

The Christian should also be concerned that he or she not be duped. The term "national security" relates to a definite area of government responsibility. And it involves activities of the utmost importance to the safety of this nation. But it has also been expanded so broadly at times that it has been used to justify activities that were only very tenuously related to national defense and to justify secrecy regarding those activities. Politicians have been able to wall off whole areas of politics in the name of national security. That sort of short-circuiting of democracy must be recognized for what it is.

But just as dangerous is the sensationalism of the media. The whole CIA is not guilty of subversion abroad, lying to Congress and spying on the American public. The appropriate efforts to uncover illegal activities at home should not justify public exposure of the whole intelligence gathering apparatus and by so doing cripple its effectiveness in necessary areas.

Democracy, Morality and Policy

In this chapter and chapter four we have reviewed the men and institutions that make foreign and military policy. Some conclusions seem clear. First, policy decisions are based not only on the merits of the problem and the policy but also on a bureaucratic struggle for influence. Decisions are not only rational but also emotional, based not only on objective analysis but also on self-interest among men and institutions.

Second, the policy leaders are dealing primarily with issues of power politics. There is no Department of Peace, no Agency for World Community, no Bureau for Human Rights. Does that mean the policy-making process screens out such considerations and raises only issues of power politics to the top level of the government? No. The president and his advisers determine the kind of issues with which they will deal. Their preferences influence the priority they assign to different kinds of issues. If Christians are concerned that such human and world community issues are not receiving adequate attention, they should become involved in efforts to change that structure of priorities. Suggestions on what Christians can do are discussed in the last chapter.

Third, there is no such thing as the foreign policy of the American people. Neither the people nor their congressional representative nor the president are fully in control of the making of foreign policy. The policy-making process is complex and the men and institutions involved in the process vary in their influence over time and as issues change.

Should the Congress or the president be in control of foreign policy? As a representative of the people, congressional decisions cannot be determined by the popularity of particular policies. Congress cannot act simply as a tool of public opinion. Neither the public nor the Congress are sources of infallible foreign policy wisdom. But neither are the president nor his advisers. They may have more information and expertise than the public or Congress, but they also make mistakes and distort policy for bureaucratic reasons.

Who should make policy? Both! The Founding Fathers of this nation understood that no one person or group of people could be trusted to always be right. So they built a government of separate branches sharing power. And so it should be.

Having said that, I must hasten to add that some reforms are certainly desirable. The Congress would do well to reform its committee system. Consideration of foreign policy is split among too many committees. Congressional oversight should be enlarged and simplified. And the selection of key committee leaders should emphasize expertise rather than aged minds and bodies.

The executive branch needs to find a way to unify itself to minimize bureaucratic self-interest. Interdepartmental committees composed of ambassadors from sovereign departments will only make good policy in spite of themselves. There should be a central authority under the president that can bind the departments together and infuse them with a common purpose.

There must be this increased unity and cooperation to insure legal and moral control of policy and action. Without them, policy can too easily slip out of the bounds of purpose and restraint, prudence and proportionality.

Questions and Answers

Q. How can all of this bargaining and compromising happen in the bureaucracy? Doesn't the president control the bureaucracy?

A. He has legal authority over it, but his control is not like that of a commander in the Army. The president can command that some certain action be done, but the independence of the bureaucracy allows it to obstruct, delay and reinterpret the orders. Thus the president commands but does not control.

Besides the independence of the bureaucrats, the president is just too busy to know everything the bureaucracy is doing or fighting about, and he is too important to have to be the one to settle interdepartmental squabbles. In the last few administrations it has been the job of the president's personal adviser on foreign affairs—MacGeorge Bundy for Kennedy, Walt Rostow for Johnson and Henry Kissinger for Nixon—to be the "eyes and ears" for the president in the bureaucracy, by checking on programs, monitoring disputes, pressing for action, evaluating recommendations and so on.

Q. I can't see how you can approve of the "cloak-and-dagger" work of the CIA.

A. I believe that the absence of war does not mean the absence of crucial, strategic, even decisive struggles between nations. War and peace are not absolute dichotomies; competition and struggle for advancement is the normal state of affairs. Thus, I cannot simply write off such strategic services simply because they occur during times of peace. Their success may actually prevent a much larger involvement later on by aborting a possible major crisis.

However, I do believe such operations must be carried out within the boundaries of moral action I have mentioned in chapter three. Because they are secret does not mean they are uninhibited by constraints of morality as well as prudence.

Q. You put a lot of faith in diplomacy, yet look how

much we lost at Yalta. We lost our shirt by trying to negotiate with the Russians.

A. Space prevents full treatment of that topic, but it is a valid one to raise. At Yalta the allies agreed that Russia would enter the war against Japan and receive in return certain islands taken from Russia by Japan in 1904. At the time, the United States was facing the need to begin planning an invasion of Japan which the American military was estimating would cost two hundred thousand American casualties. No one knew for sure if the atomic bomb would work or even lead to a surrender if it did work. So the deal was made in order to decrease the anguish of finishing the war with Japan.

Second, the agreements concerned the boundaries and government of Poland. Poland had been a part of Russia prior to World War 1, but Russia was defeated by Germany in that war and the nation of Poland was created out of former Russian territory. During World War 2 Russia was determined to get back that land and to create a buffer ring that would seal off the Russian heartland from another European invasion like Napoleon's or Hitler's. The U.S. concern was to preserve allied unity because Hitler was still not beaten. Therefore, the leaders agreed to new borders that gave part of Poland to Russia and part of Germany to Poland in return. The leaders also agreed that the government operating in Poland was to be "reorganized" by including some other Polish leaders. But the effect was marginal at best, and the agreement only accepted the existing government.

Now in effect, Russia got Poland. But we never had it. Russia was occupying it as it forced back the Germans out of Russia. Some other outcome in Poland would have required a U.S. invasion of Poland to fight the Russians, in effect the beginning of a World War 3, but we were still fighting Nazis in our effort to invade Germany and end the war. In reality, the map of Europe would look exactly the same as it does today if there had never been a Yalta Conference. At Yalta, the location of military forces, the hostile images, and the continuing struggle with Germany all prevented diplomacy from working.

Q. What about Munich then?

A. Munich was unrealistic, a complete misreading of Hitler. Munich is where the "cookie-pushers" rejected the use of force and were up against a madman and didn't know it. If Yalta reflects how military power can deadlock diplomacy, and the 1974 Middle East negotiations reflect how a balance of power can facilitate negotiations, Munich reflects how diplomacy can lead to disaster if it rejects a partnership with power.

Basic Readings

Allison, Graham. *Essence of Decision*. Boston: Little-Brown. 1971. The author explores the decision-making process at the time of the Cuban Missile Crisis from three different perspectives: rational decision-making, organizational processes and bureaucratic politics.

Destler, I. M. *Presidents, Bureaucrats and Foreign Policy*. Princeton: Princeton University Press. 1972.

Hilsman, Roger. *To Move a Nation*. New York: Delta Books. 1964. Hilsman provides an insider's view of bureaucratic politics during the Kennedy Administration. A "must" for understanding policy-making.

Irish, Marian D. and Elke Frank. *U.S. Foreign Policy*. New York: Harcourt, Brace, Jovanovich. 1975. This is a first-rate introductory text to U.S. foreign policy.

Marchetti, Victor and John D. Marks. *The CIA and the Cult of Intelligence*. New York: Alfred A. Knopf. 1974.

Sapin, Burton. *The Making of United States Foreign Policy*. New York: Frederick A. Praeger. 1966.

Simpson, Smith. *Anatomy of the State Department*. Boston: Beacon Press. 1967.

United States Senate. Committee on Foreign Relations. *CIA Foreign and Domestic Activities*. Washington, D.C.: Government Printing Office. 1975.

VI
POWER
PURPOSE
& POLICY

*"Is not this the fast that I choose: to loose the bonds
of wickedness, to undo the thongs of the yoke, to let
the oppressed go free, and to break every yoke? Is it not to
share your bread with the hungry, and bring the homeless
poor into your house . . . ?"*
Isaiah 58:6-7

Power. One indisputable fact about the United States is its
power.

Chronicles of history will always give major place to
names that symbolize the creation of that power—Pittsburg, Chicago and Detroit; Huntington, Rockefeller and
Carnegie; Eisenhower, Patton and MacArthur; the Atomic
Energy Commission, the National Aeronautics and Space
Administration and the Central Intelligence Agency.
Time would fail me to tell the stories of GM, of ITT, of Ford,
of Meany, of Luce. These men and organizations subdued
the wilderness, conquered outer space, shut the mouths of
foreign tyrants, wrought marvels of science and technology, and established mighty industrial centers and an
unequaled standard of living. And in so doing they

achieved their goal of making America the greatest power in the world.

But power is not just a goal. It is also a tool. With its power America can achieve many dreams and ambitions, hopes and goals. But which ones? What should America try to do in world affairs? Is there a moral foreign policy which America could and should follow?

But first, what do we mean by a "moral foreign policy"? Is there such a policy and should we even want to try to achieve it?

These questions are important because many scholars and statesmen deny the desirability of a moral foreign policy. They paint a grim portrait of a policy determined by moral considerations. They believe an individual may decide to apply the Sermon on the Mount to his own life, turning the other cheek, loving an enemy, not resisting evil, but a nation cannot apply those standards to its foreign policy. If it tried, either its own military leaders would take over the government and change the policy or the nation would be subdued and exploited by adversaries. An American leader decides not just for himself but for over 200 million Americans and their nation.

These scholars, who call themselves realists, also argue that the complexity of foreign and defense issues cannot be sufficiently simplified to be able to be related to abstract principles of morality. To try will put U.S. diplomats at a distinct disadvantage in dealings with subtle and devious adversaries. Finally, these scholars are critical of moralistic leaders, claiming they are rigid, arrogant, fanatical and given to airs of superiority. These attitudes supposedly promote tensions, suspicions and conflict rather than cooperation and reconciliation.

Given these limitations realists, as we saw in chapter three, advocate a dual morality. The Sermon on the Mount should be retained for individuals, but nations should operate according to a different code of behavior, one that centers around the concept of the national interest.

The realists are essentially correct in their criticisms, but their conclusion that morality should not guide foreign affairs is incorrect. The national interest is not an adequate substitute for morality because it is objective and clearly definable only on very theoretical levels. The national interest of the United States includes self-preservation, security and well being. What those interests mean about appropriate relations with Russia and Egypt, about the design cf military forces, or about levels and types of involvement in Latin America are open to controversy.

It is difficult to differentiate national interests from special interests and to be confident about the rationality of decisions in the politically-oriented executive branch. The national interest can indeed be defined as self-preservation, security and well being. But there can be mistakes in applying these interests to specific situations, and their requirements can change in time. They are subject to judgment and estimates. The national interest reduces to political prudence. Does the national interest, the security of the United States, require fleets of assault forces like aircraft carriers in the Mediterranean Sea and the Far East? There is wide disagreement on even such a major element of American foreign policy. So in actual practice the national interest becomes simply what the leaders say it is.

Being vague, the national interest is unable to serve as a moral guide to policy and, further, its vagueness can too easily justify all sorts of proclaimed policies. The national interest does not effectively serve to limit excesses of policy and can actually be used to defend the same kind of rigidity, arrogance and fanaticism that the realists perceive in a moralistic foreign policy. The concepts of prudence and proportionality discussed in chapter three are much more workable for keeping foreign policy within moral bounds. They act to hinder arrogance and fanaticism. They recognize the necessity of operating within the logic and necessity of international politics.

There is another reason why the conclusion of the realists is incorrect. A policy of power politics neglects the pressing social and environmental issues in the world. Even if the world is not a jungle since nations normally observe the principles of prudence and proportionality, it will remain nonetheless an inhospitable world with a fragile and delicate peace in the midst of dehumanizing political forces.

There are actions and programs that can build better conditions of life and heal some of the divisions, suspicions and hostilities among the peoples of the world. The sick can be restored to health, poverty can be reduced, the hungry fed, the captives and oppressed protected, the embittered and divided reconciled. A foreign policy based on the goal of peace and the standards of prudence and proportionality is good but incomplete. That policy should be augmented with positive actions of service that apply the principles of Christian life to the activities and problems of the nations and peoples of this world.

A dual morality, therefore, should be rejected. One cannot have one code of ethics for individuals and another for national political leaders. If the claims of Christianity are true, then they must be applied to all aspects of life. Foreign policy cannot be compartmentalized and isolated from morality. Both individuals and leaders must be subject to the restraints and duties, the boundaries and hopes of Christian morality.

Is there, then, a Christian Foreign Policy? If so, is it politically feasible? Is there an immoral foreign policy? If so, is it politically necessary? These four questions will be applied to alternatives, policies and goals that America can undertake.

In chapter two we noted two general approaches to foreign policy, The Prince Approach based on the use of power, and The People's Approach based on the use of an alternative to military power. If we combine that criterion of military and nonmilitary power with two other criteria, the extent of involvement in world affairs and the relative emphasis between national goals and values and world goals and values, then we can identify seven specific policies that typify the choices before American leaders.

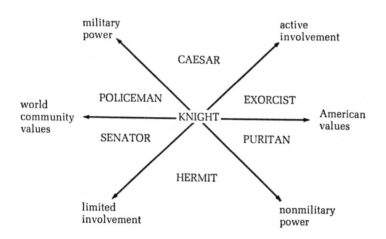

The Caesar policy seeks to build an American empire. The Exorcist works to purify the world of evil governments. The Policeman aims to resist aggressors and defend weak nations. The Senator policy is based on the power of a world political organization. The Puritan policy is founded on the power of the influence of a great American society and democracy. The Hermit policy rejects involvement in world affairs. The policy of the Knight seeks to incorporate and balance these elements.

The Caesar
The policy of the Caesar is similar to that of the Prince outlined in chapter two, so it needs only a brief discussion here. The policy lays primary emphasis on the uninhibited

use of scientific, economic and military power. It is a policy of building America into a mighty and benevolent world ruler so that, having reduced the world to submission, it could dispense justice to humanity, preserve the peace for the nations, promote greatness in the arts for world culture, and finance and train talent in science and technology for world civilization. It would be a reign of virtue. Reasonableness and fraternity would flow from the superiority of American society.

That policy would generate a great deal of satisfaction and support from many Christians. It would provide security for the nation and its people. It would reinforce the American self-image of being a blessed, chosen and superior nation and society. American foreign policy would act as the sword of the Lord against evil men and be a vehicle for the Lord to spread his blessing around the world.

Such a policy would not appear to represent a great change in the nature of the country, for it has identifiable roots in the nation's history. The emphasis on military power to achieve greatness and subdue obstacles to advancement appears to conform with American military history from the time of the War for Independence through the conquering of the Indian frontier to the liberation of Europe from Fascism. The pride in American values and the belief in their ability to uplift the rest of the world has strains from Woodrow Wilson back through Manifest Destiny, Thomas Jefferson and the Puritans.

But this is a policy with enormous dangers. The identification of American power with morality and heavenly purposes would be a breeding ground for arrogance, self-righteousness and the limitations of the Eagle Glorified position. American society has great attributes, but to assume the burden of forcing them upon other nations through military and economic domination would stimulate resistance in other nations and provoke everlasting wars for America. It would also do irreparable damage to American democracy at home.

Democracy is delicate, tenuous. It cannot exist in a nation infected with the malignant disease of divine right of action and divine truth in purpose. To try to impose one way of life on other peoples would transform American leaders into overbearing and intolerant rulers who would only too readily turn their Caesar policy on their own domestic political opponents. The American republic would follow Rome's path of degeneracy from republic to imperial dictatorship.

Fearing that the motivation and methods of the Vietnam War and the Watergate Affair reflected the early growth of such a policy, Congress undertook efforts to reassert itself in the formulation and execution of foreign policy. The War Powers Act of 1973 was enacted into law to prevent a president from involving the United States in a war without the consent of Congress, the body which has the Constitutional authority to declare war. The Budget and Impoundment Control Act of 1974, which gives Congress a more overall and complete understanding of the nation's budget, was enacted to aid the deliberation and judgment of congressmen on priorities between programs and on the appropriate funding levels for those programs. The investigations of the Watergate Affair in 1974 and the Central Intelligence Agency in 1975 were efforts to insure that government institutions and leaders were operating within the confines of the law and public policy.

The Exorcist

An Exorcist has the power to cast demons and evil forces out of people. Such a person wages war on the forces of evil and defeats them, bringing freedom and healing in their place. That role is open to America.

Chapter two discussed how foreign policy can be based on the beliefs and values of its people, and how those values and standards act as criteria for judging other nations. Those social values could be used then to identify wicked governments and evil nations. The military might of the

U.S. could then be used to rid the world of them and thus bring more freedom, safety and democracy to the world. It was this attitude that motivated Churchill to declare that England was going to fight Hitler until "every trace of Hitler's footsteps, every stain of his infected and corroding fingers will be sponged and purged and, if need be, blasted from the surface of the earth."

It was the same kind of motivation that led the American Secretary of State John Foster Dulles to proclaim American policy to be the "liberation" of Eastern Europe and the "roll back" of communism. It is the same motivation that leads many liberals today to call for American efforts to oppose if not overthrow military dictatorships.

The Exorcist would place America in the forefront of opposition to evil, leaving no doubt about its relationship to the forces of justice. Wicked nations would come to fear America and, as a Chaplain to the U.S. Senate put it, the flash of its righteous sword. It would be acting, in the Apostle Paul's image in Romans 13, as the sword of the Lord.

But who will decide what nations are moral and which are immoral and evil? And what criteria will be used? How are our leaders to determine which nations should have the right to exist and which should be "blasted" from the earth?

These questions were easy for Churchill because the Nazi race policy was combined with a war policy to destroy England, thereby adding threat to wickedness. But what if a supposedly wicked regime poses no threat? Should we declare war on them? If not, then the policy ceases to be based on moral considerations and is diluted to simple political prudence.

Less stringent measures could be used. The U.S. could equip and finance insurgent forces as it did successfully against the regime in Guatemala in 1954 and unsuccessfully against Castro in 1961. It could finance domestic turmoil and strife to try to force a change in leadership as it did with its efforts to "destabilize" the nation of Chile in 1972. We could also withdraw support of a regime as a kind of signal to its internal opponents, which we used successfully against the regime of President Diem in South Vietnam in 1963 but unsuccessfully against the military regime of Peru in the same year.

If we do undertake such efforts, then we violate the basic principle of sovereignty which characterizes nations and which is enshrined in documents signed by America. One of these, the Charter of the Organization of American States, reads in part, "No State or group of States has the right to intervene, directly or indirectly, for any reason whatever, in the internal or external affairs of any other State."

Success in any of these efforts also raises the problem of American responsibility to the new regime that comes into power. What if it turns as sour as its predecessor? And what if, after much killing and destruction in the effort to overthrow a regime, the effort fails? Can we as a foreign nation simply wash our hands like Pontius Pilate? This consideration was a heavy burden on President John F. Kennedy after the failure of the American backed invasion of Cuba in 1961.

An interventionist policy entangles American lives and honor in multiple affairs around the world. It raises disturbing moral questions itself. It carries strong dangers of self-righteousness and rigidity. It is, in short, a superficially moral policy with great political dangers for the nation.

The Policeman

American presidents since World War 2, directing the destiny of the world's most powerful nation, have proclaimed that this enormous power created a special responsibility, a special obligation to protect weak nations from agressors. This role, what President Kennedy called the "watchman on the walls of world freedom," was America's special burden and glory. It was a burden because it was costly, requiring high taxes, large armies based overseas and diversion of attention from problems at home. But this Policeman's role was also America's glory and road to greatness. It made America the chief bulwark against the flood of communism, the defender of the weak and the leader of all free nations.

How does a nation play the role of Policeman? Three general ways are possible. First, it may simply dominate the rest of the world. The United States has had a sphere of influence in Latin America since the early 1900s. We have protected that area from outside nations on the basis of the Monroe Doctrine. President Monroe stated that Latin America was not open to colonization by European nations and we would oppose any European nation that tried to take over a Latin American country. But President Theodore Roosevelt expanded the Monroe Doctrine through the so-called Roosevelt Corollary. It states that when violence and turmoil occur within a Latin American nation or when a European nation has a case against a Latin American nation for defaulting on debt or whatever, the United States had the right to intervene in the situation and take over the Latin American nation to restore order and tranquility or to administer the punishment for the European nation. This, Roosevelt declared in his State of the Union message in 1904, was the legitimate exercise by the United States of "an international police power."

The Monroe Doctrine and its Roosevelt Corollary could be applied worldwide to prevent aggression and abort revolutions and civil war in other nations. This would require military superiority over any and every other nation, as well as the wealth, strength and will to intervene anywhere around the world to protect borders or restore order. America would not rule the world, but it would have protectorates everywhere. Only those changes in politics which are acceptable to the United States would be allowed. Within those rules of change, the nations could go about their business of development and progress. America would be Atlas, holding up the world, bearing the burden and achieving a greatness that comes from protecting the weak, defeating the wrong and making progress possible.

A second way of acting as Policeman is to form an alliance system with all those nations that need protection against enemies. The United States would agree that it would come to the aid of any alliance member in danger. The key portion of these alliance agreements read much like this paragraph from the NATO Treaty:

> The Parties agree that an armed attack against one or more of them in Europe or North America shall be considered an attack against them all; and consequently they agree that, if such an armed attack occurs, each of them ... will assist the Party or Parties so attacked by taking forthwith, individually and in concert with the other Parties, such action as it deems necessary, including the use of armed force, to restore and maintain the security of the North Atlantic area.

If a new Hitler arose, he would have no cause to think, as did the German leaders of World War 1 and World War 2, that the United States might not become involved. America, through the alliance system, would put itself on record that it would immediately come to the aid of any member in danger. And though America might act by itself as it did in 1965 in Vietnam and the Dominican Republic, it could also act in concert with its alliance partners as it did many other times.

A third possible method of acting as world Policeman is to work out an arrangement with Russia to combine forces against the radicals and revolutionaries promoting trouble in the underdeveloped areas of the world. Instead of remaining adversaries the two super nations would become partners and forge a common front against the hostility and turbulence in Asia, Africa and Latin America which are being caused by the pressures of growing famine and booming population.

Another possible motivation for such an arrangement is this: If the two nations could compromise their differences to the point of being able to cooperate, then they would reduce the danger to themselves and escape the costly necessity of constant competition all around the globe. And then, like a couple of mafia leaders, they could carve out "territories" for themselves and enforce mutually beneficial economic and political arrangements.

America undertook this Policeman's role for two decades after World War 2, using a combination of the first two methods. And that role was useful and important for some of the world's nations. Some of them escaped invasion and others received help in resistance when invasion occurred. Other nations escaped high self-defense burdens and were able to concentrate on internal development. Japan and West Germany used the U.S. nuclear shield for such an advantage.

The forging of defensive alliances among allies introduced economies of scale and reduced the duplication and waste of numerous independent forces. It also provided a coherent and unified military front, inhibited the spread of nuclear weapons to other countries and reduced reaction time in an emergency. Because the United States undertook this role of world policeman, Europe and Japan have rebuilt their societies from the ruin of World War 2, the movement of the Russian empire was halted in Europe and frustrated elsewhere around the globe, and the great historical movement of decolonization proceeded remarkably smooth and unhindered.

But heavy burdens and compromise have also flowed from this policy. The financial requirements for worldwide defense have been high, regularly eating up one-half of total government spending. Taxes have had to be high, and balance of payments have been distorted by so much U.S. money being spent overseas.

And countries America wanted to save for freedom were saved from communism but degenerated into other kinds of dictatorships anyway. South Korea, the Philippines, Brazil, Chile, Greece, Nicaragua and Portugal have been members of the so-called Free World, but their peoples have not been free. Many times their freedoms were extinguished with the use of guns and tanks given or sold to their leaders by the U.S. The original purpose and desire of American policy toward these countries have been lost as ambitious colonels have taken the tools of American policy and used them for their own personal power. Thus the greatness of the American policy has been tarnished in the eyes of thousands of persons for whom America shouldered the burden of worldwide defense.

American domestic society has not escaped the impact of this Policeman role either. Its industrial economy has become heavily dependent upon defense contracts. Its schools, churches, and news media have been mobilized to support the military and its policies. Summit meetings overseas regarding lands far away have substituted for summit meetings in Chicago and Pittsburg and Los Angeles regarding pressing problems in American domestic social life.

The Senator
The next two alternative policies involve a de-emphasis on military power and a commitment to other forms of power. The Senator emphasizes the use of American diplomatic and economic power within the United Nations to build a world community where military power is restrained or unnecessary.

This option is not necessarily the same as The People's Approach of Woodrow Wilson because the Senator does not require all nations to be republics and does not rely on a projected world public opinion to supplant military power. This approach accepts nations as they are but assumes that great amounts of American economic and diplomatic power can make possible international programs that will meet pressing international needs, can forge coalitions of cooperation that will reconcile disputes and relieve tensions, and can make America a major international statesman, or Senator, in the world organization. It would reject acting alone around the world or in partnership only with close allies. It would accept the status of being a member of a world community and restrict the use of its power to conform to the decisions of that community.

This policy does not assume the development of a world government. It only assumes a rebirth of workability in the United Nations. The U.N. was created at the end of World War 2 to enforce a collective security arrangement for peace, to regulate the governing of colonies on their path to independence, and to promote economic and social progress. Toward those ends a Charter, or a kind of constitution, was drafted.

A study of the U.N. could easily run into volumes, and space obviously precludes doing that now. Instead, three major features about the U.N. which affect the appropriateness of a Senator Policy for the United States will be identified.

The first such feature is the impotence of the organization in peace keeping. The U.N. was built upon the assumption that cooperation among the Great Powers that had characterized their wartime experience would continue. But after the war the world divided between the American allies and the Russian allies. The veto was used in the Security Council to prevent any action from being taken. The one time the Security Council escaped that deadlock occurred at the beginning of the Korean War. The Russia representative had walked out of the Security Council over another issue, and while he was gone, North Korea opened its attack and the Security Council responded by creating a collective security force under the command of the United States and led by General Douglas MacArthur. The Russian delegate came running back and has not left since.

With the U.N. hampered in its peace keeping functions

once again, the United States proposed, in effect, a constitutional revision. It introduced and the U.N. accepted the "Uniting for Peace Resolution" which allows the General Assembly to take action when the Security Council cannot or will not act to keep the peace. This was a convenient development for the United States because its European and Latin American allies gave it an automatic majority.

A second major feature of the United Nations is its enlarged membership. There were 56 original members, but now 135 nations belong. That has brought pressure for new orientations in U.N. activities and has eliminated the automatic American majority. Whereas the Americans saw the U.N. primarily for peace keeping, the new nations have seen it primarily for furthering decolonization and for providing organizations and resources for economic development. New committees and commissions have developed out of these new concerns. A long list of resolutions and declarations passed by the General Assembly have placed the U.N. firmly on the side of those nations seeking the end of colonialism, apartheid, racial and sexual discrimination, and economic exploitation between the industrial nations and the underdeveloped nations.

A third feature of the U.N. is the gap between the voting majority and the actual international distribution of political and economic power. Many of the resolutions adopted remain rhetoric because the nations committed to them are unable to put them into effect. This has led to increasing exasperation by the new nations and has turned the General Assembly into a platform for tirades and an agent for world change.

All this has left the nations which provide the major financial support of the U.N. very disturbed—France calling the General Assembly sessions "scandalous" and the United States voicing fears about a "tyranny of the majority." The United States previously financed over 31% of the U.N. budget, but in recent years it has cut that back to

25%, while France and Russia have refused to pay their shares of the costs of operations and programs they oppose.

The world is simply still too fractured and divided for an American effort to develop a world community to be successful. Cleavages are too deep to be bridged, policies are too divergent to be reconciled, and suspicions and ambitions are too vast to be subdued.

The United Nations is important and useful. If it did not exist, some similar organization would have to be created to sponsor and supervise the inescapable work done by many of its international committees and commissions. It promotes cooperation on everything from police investigations (Interpol) to health research (World Health Organization) to mail service (Universal Postal Union). It has dampened conflicts in the Middle East and elsewhere. It has garnered international support for U.S. actions as in the 1962 Cuban Missile Crisis. So the U.N. should not, in fact, cannot be rejected.

But neither should it be the sole or even the primary vehicle through which America operates its foreign policy. America has needs and supports conditions of world order far beyond the perspectives of some of the new nations. And the world is still too fragile and chaos still too close to the surface for voting equality and international majoritarianism to be viable means toward world order.

The policy of acting as a world Senator has appealing aspects associated with it, aspects like the "rule of law," the primacy of reason and debate over power politics, and the concern with the development and protection of fundamental human rights. So again, the U.N. ought not be rejected.

The Puritan
If a world organization like the U.N. falls short of its promise, if it is too devoid of the right kind of power and too entangling for the well-being of America, one still need

not be resigned to rely exclusively on military power. Many Americans would recommend reliance on the reputation of good deeds and a good name for influence in a corrupt world.

One thread woven into the fabric of the American heritage can be traced as far back as the Puritans. This thread emphasizes integrity as reflected in a moral and enlightened society. The Founding Fathers of the nation had a clear conception of America as a new nation, one that had escaped all the corruption and vices of Europe. These early patriots saw themselves building a new kind of society, one that matched the longings of all the repressed peoples of the world. This new society in the new world would so attract the peoples and leaders of the world that America would soon hold enormous moral influence, and nations would soon begin to try to copy the American experience. America would be a lighthouse on a hill, a beacon to the world.

That view has special attraction to millions of Americans today who are caught in the grip of urban blight, spiraling crime and drug abuse, and revelations of dishonesty in government. These Americans would like to see the primary emphasis of the American government's activities directed inward, reconstructing the deteriorated areas of America and bringing new hope to its peoples.

With its own home affairs cleaned up and its citizens living in righteousness and reconciliation, America could give a rebirth to democracy around the world. America could face the world's tyrants and condemn their policies and demand reforms in the name of their peoples and universal justice. President Kennedy, for example, gave extra weight to his criticism of communist repression when he told the United Nations:

> Through legislation and administrative action, through moral and legal commitment, this government has launched a determined effort to rid our nation of discrimination which has existed too long—in education,

in housing, in transportation, in employment, in the
Civil Service, in recreation and in places of public accommodation. And, therefore, in this or any other for-
um, we do not hesitate to condemn racial or religious
injustice, whether committed or permitted by friend or
foe.

When America has cleansed itself of injustice, banished
the clouds of smog, rebuilt the barrios and slums of the
cities, and rekindled the spirit of liberty and democracy,
then America will have a power sharper than the sword of
two-bit colonels and dictators running countries in Asia,
Africa and Latin America. America will have more influence and power in the United Nations and in international
conferences than it ever had with its fleets of bombers
coupled with congested cities, or with its missiles and
tanks coupled with discrimination and injustice.

Or will it?

When William Shirer, author of *The Rise and Fall of the
Third Reich*, asked Germans why they did nothing to re-
trieve their liberty from Hitler in the 1930s, he was answered with, "What could we do?" The Gestapo and other
secret police organizations were crawling throughout Germany, the government controlled the newspapers, motion
pictures, schools, and even the churches. No meetings by
opponents were possible to develop actions or even to coordinate activities. Germans may have longed for the freedom of America, but they could not achieve it by simply
desiring it, and Hitler was not about to give it to them.
Nor was Stalin or Khrushchev. Even friendship with
America is not causing South Africa to cease its policies of
apartheid or the Arabs to call off their opposition to Israel.

Justice and democracy are prized possessions of American citizens, but they are not powerful forces in world
politics. They embody the hopes and aspirations of millions of the world's peoples, but they are powerless to
break the bonds of repression in other countries. A great
society is not a goal Americans want to abandon. But it is

not a goal to be sought instead of military power. Both must be sought together if America is to remain both a democracy and a world leader. The analysis in chapter two remains valid—power, understood in terms of physical might, is the core feature of world politics. And there is no other substitute.

The Hermit

We come now to an important question. If America cannot use its military power to achieve great moral goals, and if there are no effective substitutes for military power, why not just forget the world and leave the nations to their own fates? Why not bring American soldiers home from far-flung bases and divert tax monies from weapons of destruction to programs of social betterment? And instead of forcing itself into other people's problems and getting tangled up in international tensions and conflicts, why not just come home and be free of world problems?

The assumption underlying this sentiment is that we can escape the troubles of the world, that by leaving the rest of the world alone, they will leave us alone. And separated from the rest of the world by immense oceans, this isolationist dream seems more applicable to the U.S. than any other nation. Why not be like Canada or Mexico and just stay home?

This isolationist urge is a policy that has a hidden cost— our standard of living. The American economy would collapse if we cut ourselves off from the rest of the world. And we cannot escape the world's troubles and conflicts by simply being a nation of commercial traders. From the War of 1812 through World War 2 our economic interests in overseas markets have brought us into inescapable involvement with other nations' foreign policies and wars.

When President Thomas Jefferson tried to allow trade with both England and France during the Napoleonic Wars, those two nations would not allow it. When he tried to escape war with them by closing American shipping to

Europe a depression hit the Northeast part of the country. And the war came in 1812 despite his policy. So unless the American people are willing to trade their present standard of living with that of Mexico, or unless they are willing to place themselves under the protection and economic dependence of another great nation (as Canada has with the United States), they cannot escape the world.

And beyond that, the oceans are no longer great barriers to protect this nation. The development of long-range bombers and intercontinental missiles has robbed the seas of their strategic significance in terms of our protection. We cannot get away.

So the role of the hermit, living a simple life far away from the toils and troubles of the world, is not possible for this nation in today's world. We may want to follow the policy advocated by George Washington and stay out of entangling alliances with other countries. But as Adlai Stevenson reminded us, George Washington wrote by the light of a candle and traveled by horse and buggy.

Bicentennial America
Is America, then, having just celebrated its 200th birthday, condemned as just another tired nation caught in the web of power politics? Is there no hope for any moral content and purpose in American foreign policy, no hope that America can have some special moral role to play in the world today as it did 200 years ago?

Yes, there is hope. On the basis of this and other chapters we can answer that America can and, therefore, should have a morally purposeful foreign policy.

But do not assume it will be easy. Here and in chapter two we have seen that while no immoral policy is necessary, neither is any purely moral policy politically possible. And while a dual morality is not acceptable, neither is it necessary.

Morality can be applied to foreign policy in two ways. First, through such principles as prudence and propor-

tionality, it can minimize the undesirable aspects of foreign policy and prevent it from becoming immoral. Beyond that, moral concerns should be geared into foreign
policy so that the policy will be directed toward serving
the desperate needs of people as well as the needs and
interests of the nation.

For this last policy I would present the image of the
Knight. This image comes out of the Middle Ages and has
become highly romanticized, but it nevertheless presents
those essential characteristics that should typify American foreign policy.

One characteristic of the Knight is that he is a warrior.
And we need to recognize that military power, while undesirable, is unavoidable. Military power will remain indispensable for the protection of America and its allies.
And the balance of power, measured predominately in
terms of military power, will remain the foundation of a
constructed peace and stability, and thereby the prerequi-
site for any attempts to improve the condition of the world.

There will remain choices and disagreements regarding
the appropriate size of American military forces and the
types of weapons. But at a minimum I would like to see
America include the following in its military policy: (a) a
no-first use principle for nuclear weapons; (b) preservation of an assured second-strike capability; and (c) the development of new strategies to make limited war effective.
The goals of limited war, as outlined in chapter four, need
to be achieved and maintained.

Another characteristic of the Knight is his "shining
armor." That shining armor should represent the justice
and integrity of American society. We must be a nation
where men and women of different races and lifestyles can
work together in equality and peace to enrich their lives
and improve their communities and nation. This is desirable in itself, but is also desirable in terms of strengthening
American positions on world issues with moral overtones.

The knights in the legendary King Arthur's Court were

members of the King's Round Table. Issues were discussed there, actions coordinated and cooperation forged. America must pursue a similar policy of membership and cooperation in world organizations.

The world today is far different from the bipolar world of the 1950s. The two super nations no longer dominate the rest of the world. Europe and Japan have rebuilt their strength, the Middle East has discovered the power potential of oil and former alliances are breaking down. Except for the American and Russian nuclear arsenals (which cannot be used effectively for political purposes), the world is the home of great but relatively equal and deeply interdependent nations. The possibility of energy independence for America is looking increasingly dim. Russia cannot grow enough wheat for its citizens. The Middle East must adopt Western technology and industrialize itself before its oil supplies run out or it will be reduced to impoverished deserts. In this setting, an American attempt to remain independent and dominate would have as much success as that symbol of foolishness, the knight Don Quixote.

To discuss cooperation is to imply purpose. The purposes of international cooperation today are clear—to deal with world issues like human rights, famine and terrorism.

Knights tried to identify themselves or their reputations with emblems on their shields. America needs an identification too, an indentification with justice and dedication to people.

World politics today must involve more than traditional statecraft. World peace will continue to rest on a geopolitical balance of power, but that will be an increasingly insufficient foundation to preserve the peace if the conditions of life continue to deteriorate throughout the world. But beyond that, the value of the individual human person has been lost in the statecraft of today. The purpose of international politics was to protect the nation, for it was assumed that when the nation was safe and prosperous, the people would be safe and happy. But those human purposes have been lost under the pressures of the twentieth century.

Balance of power politics must be strongly supplemented with a rededication to the values and conditions of people. It is true that American foreign policy cannot be geared to the transformation of other societies. But the American government can move on two levels to give action. On the international level it can strengthen its commitment and support of institutions and programs that serve human needs, such as the World Health Organization, the United Nations Human Rights Commission, and the United Nations High Commissioner for Refugees. Additionally, America could take the lead in the creation of new institutions like a World Food Bank.

On the national level America could adopt policies to strengthen its commitment to people. Just as it has adopted a national energy-conservation program, so the government could adopt a national food-conservation program and couple that with a massive new effort at increasing food production for export. The government could also adopt a renewed commitment to speak the truth about the conditions of life around the world, not letting nations hide mass starvation as Ethiopia did, or hide prisons full of political prisoners as many nations do today. An enlarged damage-limitation policy could also be adopted into American military policy, emphasizing those weapons and strategies that would minimize the destruction of lives and agricultural areas.

In legends, knights went about the land slaying dragons. The dragons of this world—the Four Horsemen if you will—are not legendary. If the Lord should delay his return another twenty-five years (if not more), consider the lives that could be saved and sufferings alleviated if America would adopt this rededication to human value. And what might be achieved in implementing such a policy as this? America could convince other great powers to join it and lay the foundation of another great legitimizing principle in world affairs—the establishment of a minimum standard of world justice.

Questions and Answers

Q. You are saying that there is no such thing as a Christian foreign policy?

A. Yes, that's right.

Q. Then how can you argue against two moralities? How can Christianity be applied if there is no Christian foreign policy?

A. I have been arguing that there is no simple and easy answer. There is no ready-made policy package waiting to be applied.

Instead, I have been arguing that it is possible to develop a policy that is acceptable or tolerable to Christian concerns. I will not claim that a policy is a moral policy, but if it is morally acceptable then I believe Christians can fulfill their civic obligations in good conscience.

Such a position accepts power and war. I don't like either one, but they are both inescapable. But because they are inescapable does not mean I have to consider them moral. War is not moral. War may be necessary. War is always tragic—and so we need to be concerned with building the foundation for peace. But so long as power, purposes and policies are kept within the bounds of prudence and proportionality, then I believe they must be considered morally acceptable.

Now beyond that, an acceptable foreign policy must comprise more than just power politics. It must also incorporate programs that are designed, in the words of a former president, "to heal and to build." These programs operate to serve the needs of people within the structure of peace that power politics supports. The term "statecraft" implies that power is employed for the sole benefit of the state and perhaps its own citizens. But for Christians there must be human ends of power as well as state goals.

Q. Your conception of the Knight in shining armor—would it not lead to an attitude of smug superiority? What will keep the Knight from becoming a Crusader?

A. The Knight is not a perfect model, but there is no perfect model because there is no single policy that is right. I chose the Knight as a model because it is a composite of elements like military power, personal integrity, concern for justice and a willingness to work in a group. Now the Knight is not absolutely pure, none of these elements is achieved completely. But all should be present and work to balance each other. The military power is not emphasized to the point of becoming a Caesar, the concern for justice is not emphasized to the point of becoming an Exorcist, the willingness to work in a group is not emphasized to the point of becoming a world Senator, and so on. This model of a multi-faceted but balanced policy is my conception of a desirable policy. Then individuals can work within this framework to support or change specific policies and programs that they see to be appropriate.

Basic Readings

Bloomfield, Lincoln. *In Search of American Foreign Policy*. New York: Oxford University Press. 1974.

Claude, Inis. *The Changing United Nations*. New York: Random House. 1967.

Liska, George. *War and Order*. Baltimore: The Johns Hopkins University Press. 1968.

Tucker, Robert. *Nation or Empire*. Baltimore: The Johns Hopkins University Press. 1968.

VII
ROLES
WORTHY OF
OUR CALLING

*"I therefore, a prisoner for the Lord, beg you
to lead a life worthy of the calling to which you
have been called."*
Ephesians 4:1

This book has not been about the Hawk and the Dove, the relative merits of promilitary and antimilitary approaches to foreign policy. Nor has it been about the Eagle and the Bear, the relative merits of Russian-American disputes and detente. It has been about the Christian living in two worlds, a citizen of two kingdoms, symbolized by the Eagle of American power and might and the Dove of the Spirit and will of Christ. And those two worlds operate on different principles.

Christians bring to their view of world affairs certain beliefs and attitudes derived from their faith. One is the majesty and sovereignty of God over men and nations. From that flows our attitude toward God as our possessor and dispossessor. Constantly and ultimately our lives are to be lived for him and according to his precepts.

Another feature of the Christian life is the law of love. From God's commandment of love and from our communion with him comes a lifestyle of love to be lived out among the people of this world. We are to love others—our brother and our enemy.

A third feature is a life of witness and service. We cannot hide our life in Christ under a rock or drown it in the cares and concerns of this life. We are to be a witness to the rest of the world of God's redeeming, sustaining, and guiding mercy and power. Flowing from our love and witness should be service to the needs of others. Whether as a "suffering servant" or an authoritarian hero image, we have before us as a teaching guide the model of the Good Samaritan.

But when Christians view the world of international politics, they see a world of radically different principles. They see a world of dispersed and unequal power, a world in which a nation finds security only in military forces that can defend it or in alliance with a greater nation which can and will. This concern with security restricts primary interest to one's own nation. This narrowing scope of concerns is required by, but also preserves, the international struggle.

Out of the diversity of nations and peoples come Princes with overblown ambitions and Prophets seeking to remake portions of the globe by force. Out of the diversity of resources and cultures come plagues like famine and poverty, further warping the ideals and goals of leaders and peoples. Yet also, thankfully, out of that struggle among nations come opportunities for peace and progress, opportunities to reduce tragedy and enhance well-being.

In this political world of danger and opportunity America, with its immense economic and military power, has numerous alternatives in goals, strategies and programs, some of which can make the world safer and more humane, and others of which can make it more dangerous and less hospitable to mankind. The social values of America have traditionally supported efforts to aid other peoples, sending aid to the Latin American colonies struggling to free themselves from Spanish rule in the early 1800s, sending missionaries and medical doctors around the world, and entering two world struggles and rebuilding the destroyed and bankrupt nations afterwards. But there are other factors of power and self-interest at work that warp the policy-making process even here: The distribution of power requires alliances and cooperation with undemocratic regimes; the background of our leaders elected into positions of wealth and authority make them insensitive to the depths of hatred, poverty and social cleavages in other nations; and the self-interest of government departments and bureaucrats force compromising and bargaining.

The Christian then lives in two very different worlds. While he may not be of this world, he is in it. They cannot be merged. But neither can they be compartmentalized. Yet both have far reaching demands and implications over the individual and over each other. The Christian is between them, between the sovereignty of the state and the sovereignty of God, between the Commander in Chief and the Prince of Peace, between the Eagle and the Dove.

The Aviary
The large cage in a zoo housing a collection of birds is called an aviary. In finding a place between the Eagle and the Dove, the Christian should be on guard to avoid certain kinds of birds found in the aviary of life. These birds represent pressures and attitudes to which Christians are subjected.

The ostrich is known as the bird with the curious habit of hiding by burying its head in the ground. Many persons advocate such an attitude for Christians arguing that Christians should disregard political issues, not disagree with each other about them and concentrate instead on an ab-

stract and compartmentalized study of the Scriptures ...
or to become involved in the church's programs of fun,
food and fellowship. But just as the ostrich does not escape
detection or the consequences of trouble around it by
sticking its head in the sand, so Christians will not escape
the issues and consequences of foreign policy by barring
them from discussion and study.

The turkey is the bird that concentrates on eating the
wonderful and ever abundant supply of food that is provided. The turkey devotes its time and energy to its own
comforts, its own eating pleasure, its own opportunities to
get fat. And it always ends up dead, served as some family's Thanksgiving or Christmas dinner. And again many
Christians succumb to the temptation to concentrate on
their own comfort and well-being, their own personal ambitions and financial success. They block out the warnings
that their world might collapse under the gun of a foreign
dictator if they do not pay attention to events and trends in
world politics.

The hawk represents an attitude of unscrupulous use of
power. Swooping down without warning like the crack of
doom to seize and ravage a weaker creature, the hawk is
the symbol of power glorified, of unilateral attack, of
crushing assault. Power is not to be disregarded and taken
lightly, but the hawk is a predator and so is no fit symbol
for the Christian.

The chicken is the opposite, representing advice to protect the peace by escaping danger. If nuclear weapons are
dangerous, the chicken advises abolishing them no matter
what others do with their nuclear weapons. If another
nation threatens the peace because of a certain American
policy, the chicken argues for changing that policy and for-
getting the issues involved. Peace, not the conditions that
make for lasting peace or the issues of justice and dignity,
is the sole concern of the chicken. The one-issue approach
to foreign policy is inadequate. Statesmen must balance
multiple values like peace, justice and freedom. Peace,

without the other two, is tyranny. The chicken is of the same family as the turkey and ends up either as someone else's egg-producing machine or as a dinner. The principle of love is not to be confused with the principle of the chicken. The chicken has no principles and so has nothing to defend. The ethic of love postulates the value and worth of other people, and that means they may have to be supported and defended when necessary.

The *parrot* is the bird that repeats what it is told. For that reason it is well liked. But it is also stupid. It doesn't question what it is told and, therefore, it can repeat some awful ideas. Being concerned for or aware of world affairs does not mean simply swallowing the public statements of government leaders or the media. The Pentagon Papers and the Watergate Affair have disclosed the capacity of government leaders to distort the news. And the media networks and newspaper chains are not bastions of objective reporting. So the Christian should always remain a little detached from public statements and open to divergent opinion.

The *owl* is the bird that does represent a suitable model for Christians. The owl symbolizes wisdom, the request of Solomon and the prayer of Paul for the Philippians. Wisdom is a gift of God and Christians cannot confront the issues of foreign policy and morality without the benefit of that gift. But wisdom also involves effort. It needs a foundation of knowledge and discernment.

Wisdom

What is wisdom? Who is the wise person? Wisdom is not selecting certain congenial Scripture passages or dogmatic interpretations and applying them indiscriminately to all events. Nor is the person who "pontificates" on all aspects of world affairs, drawing on his vast storehouses of ignorance, the model of the wise person.

Wisdom incorporates the insight and leadership God gives us in specific circumstances. Wisdom is not static but always fresh and current. It is also personal. We are individuals, and God deals with us as individuals with different needs and different potential contributions. Since wisdom is not absolute and eternal, it requires constant prayer and seeking the guidance of the Holy Spirit. It comes as we allow the Holy Spirit to lead us into his truth while we are facing the dilemmas of choice that the pressures and events of life force upon us. It comes from a living, purposeful God. It comes to us where we are on our journey of Christian maturity and service. It comes to meet our needs as individuals, to meet the needs of the situation and to meet the needs of God's plans.

This wisdom of leadership also involves knowledge and discernment. Continual attention to world events is not the favorite pastime of American citizens. A study found the American public divided into a pyramid of three segments.[1] The largest segment comprises the Apathetic Public. These are persons with little or no interest in the news of foreign affairs and who cannot explain the background or significance of news items. The Attentive Public comprises persons who follow the news, have some understanding of its background and importance, and discuss it with their friends. The smallest segment, the Active Public, includes persons who become involved in influencing decisions. That involvement runs from writing opinions to congressmen to the point of entering politics or government service.

The size of the three segments do change. The relative sizes of the Apathetic and Attentive Publics shift dramatically in times of crisis. National elections will again bulge the size of the Attentive Public, for they are barely able to escape news of the campaigns. But the knowledge they receive from electoral campaigns is likely to be distorted, for candidates will grossly simplify issues in order to get attention.

There are several reasons for the widespread apathy. Many people believe there are no significant differences in alternatives. Other people rest in the faith that everything will eventually turn out right. The belief is also widespread that nothing can be done to influence events or policy choices, so it is senseless to put out the effort to stay informed or become emotionally aroused and committed to a policy.

There is some truth in each of these beliefs. But there is not enough truth to justify the apathy. The average citizen cannot change the world. But, as a part of a larger group, he can have an impact on events. And the less people there are involved in shaping policy, the more significant will be the impact of those who do get involved.

Wisdom also involves discernment. Twisted visions abound throughout the land. Some are conspiratorial, including the belief that a secret group of world bankers run world affairs and caused World Wars 1 and 2 for their own profit. Other visions seem peculiarly distorted, such as the one that the State Department is filled with homosexuals. These visions have a form of reason but the substance is lacking. Verifying evidence is absent, or a cause and effect relationship is strained to the point of obsession.

Wise persons will also be aware of the distortions in political cartoons. Cartoonists help us see one side of an issue but use great distortions of other sides to be humorous. The cartoon about Department of Defense spending on page 100 is an obvious example of this kind of exaggeration and distortion. The importance is not that distortion exists. The importance is that these cartoons can create a permanently warped image in our minds that we accept as essentially accurate.

Awareness of the slants and vested interests of our sources of information is another part of wisdom. America has a free press. Very few American cities have competing newspapers, though, and the single newspaper of many cities is owned by an outside newspaper chain. Those newspaper chains normally have definite political views and perspectives. A recent book, *TV and National Defense* by Ernest Lefever, has documented the liberal slant and selective treatment of national defense news by the largest television network, CBS.

Wisdom, then, involves regular and discerning attention to news of world affairs and to the leadership of the Holy Spirit. This is not easy to do, but it is the foundation of the democratic life of rational discussion and debate. It is also the foundation for the following three roles for Christians.

Wisdom is well and good but it is not enough, just as faith without works is not enough. According to the letter of James, we must also act. Edmund Burke put it succinctly when he stated that the only thing necessary for the triumph of evil is for good people to do nothing.

What can the Christian person do about world affairs and American foreign policy? Here are three suggestions: First, like Joseph and Daniel of old, Christians can go into political and government careers. They can become the men and women who shape and move the decisions and policies of this nation. Second, Christians can act as their own CIA, or Christian Intelligence Agency. They can explore government policies and world problems from a Christian perspective. This could raise moral issues to government leaders and raise the level of awareness of the general Christian public. Third, Christians can act as the salt of the earth to reduce hostilities and promote reconciliation and harmony among people.

Remember Joseph and Daniel

The arena of public service either in a government agency or in political office should be seen as an honorable and useful career. That is not the view normally taken by Christians. The very word politician raises up images of dishonesty, corruption and amoral dealings among men. This view has been reinforced by the revelations about Congressman Hays and his secretary, Congressman Mills and his double life with a stripper, President Nixon and the

Watergate Affair and Willy Brandt's resignation as Chancellor of West Germany because of his affair with a woman who turned out to be an East German spy. This kind of revelation about men in the highest political offices in the land has left many Christians convinced that politics is no place for the Christian.

But to see just these affairs and conclude that politics is no place for a Christian is a distorted evaluation. Looked at another way, these revelations could mean that Christians are more desperately needed in politics now than ever before, both to retain authority behind the forces of good and to prevent the domination of life by an immoral government. There are good reasons why Christians should not forsake a political career just because it is infested with possibilities of immorality.

First, consider Joseph and Daniel. These young Hebrews entered government service and served God and their nation well. It could not be said that Joseph worked in a land that did not know sin and immorality. Yet he served there and by so doing saved his family, the embryo of the Hebrew nation, and part of the Middle East from starvation by famine. And famine again is becoming a world problem needing great leaders.

Consider Daniel and his friends. These young men again served in a godless nation and again did so without compromising their beliefs and principles. Early in their career they forsook the social behavior of Babylon and ate only food that was acceptable to their beliefs and proved to be the better for it. Again, when they faced a conflict between loyalty to their God and loyalty to the nation, they chose loyalty to their God—and won. Daniel escaped the lions and his three friends escaped the fire of the furnace. So immorality does not have to be a part of the life of politicians; they have no special claim on it.

Beyond the fact that government service should not be rejected because some politicians, like some car salesmen, are immoral is the fact that a Christian can be useful to

God, to his nation and to the world in government service. There are many issues of foreign policy in which a Christian could make a substantial contribution both to human welfare and world peace. He will not cherish unrealistic hopes about being able to engineer a change in the nature of man without the Holy Spirit. The regenerated and Spirit-filled life of the Christian also leads to a life of service to others. There are Christians today throughout the government—in the bureaucracy, in Congress, in the courts—finding in government work a tangible way to live out their ideal of service. And do not forget the words of Mordecai when he told Esther, "Who knoweth whether thou are come into the kingdom for such a time as this?" (Esther 4:14).

Can a Christian do anything worthwhile in a government career? Will he be listened to? Can he rise high enough to have any substantial influence? The same questions could be asked about the Christian in law or education or real estate. What a Christian can or cannot do depends upon his own abilities, the will of God, and the particular situation and forces operating in events.

There are vast amounts of disagreement among leaders themselves, so one can support those persons whose positions are closest to his. And beyond that, a person with ability in understanding, analyzing and expressing issues will be noticed and listened to. That does not mean his position will always be accepted, but it does mean he can join the policy-formulation process.

In conclusion as to whether a Christian can be a Joseph or Daniel today, I would point to Dag Hammarskjold. He was Secretary General of the United Nations between 1953 and 1961 and used that office in many ways as an international civil servant to advance the peace. He obtained the release of American airmen from Communist China in 1955, promoted mediation and dampened the fires of war in the Middle East in 1956 and 1958, and was instrumental in preventing civil war in the Congo around 1960. Immensely important work. And done by a man in deep communion with God.

In an article written after being elected Secretary General he acknowledged his commitments to a fundamental belief in God. His personal diary, titled simply *Markings*, is a history of his spiritual growth and reveals his deep dependence on God and recognition of God's involvement in his work. In an entry made at the time China announced the release of the American airmen, Hammarskjold wrote that it was God's efforts, not his, that brought it to pass. He rejoiced that God had found a use for his work.

This was Dag Hammarskjold. A man devoted and dedicated to God finding his role of service in the worldwide causes of justice and peace. Unlike Daniel and his friends, however, God did not spare Hammarskjold from a mysterious death over Africa in 1961. But his life, his work and his writings remain symbols of the possibilities open to Christians in the world of foreign policy. Government departments engaged in foreign affairs need Christians characterized by Lincoln's Second Inaugural Address, "with malice toward none; with charity for all; with firmness in the right, as God gives us to see the right...."

Rather than rejecting politics as a vocation, Christian parents, Christian colleges and the churches of America should uphold to their young people the vision of government as a place of Christian service to God, to their nation and to the world. Do not discourage a government career because of disgust with corrupt politicians. Reaffirm the need for Christians to infiltrate government and use their talents in national service. The National Association of Evangelicals sponsors each year a Washington Seminar in which Christian college students and Christians in government are brought together to discuss government operations and career potentials for young Christians. This is a valuable service to Christians and should be explored by any young person interested in government service.

A Christian CIA

A regime must have good information and analysis to be effective in its operations. Government leaders are recruited on the basis of their knowledge and expertise. That is supplemented by information from intelligence agencies like the CIA (Central Intelligence Agency) to insure that the leaders' policies are feasible and practical. The intelligence agencies' information is further supplemented by analysis from outside "think tanks" like the RAND Corporation in Santa Monica, California or the Hudson Institute in New York. Penetrating analyses of possibilities, implications, hindrances and potentials are necessary.

Christians also need information and analysis on world affairs if they are not to be a timid and apathetic ostrich, a brazen hawk, a gullible parrot or a self-deluded turkey. Dr. Dale Parnell, Chancellor of the San Diego Community Colleges, exhorted a group of young Christians to use their lives, in whatever occupation they were entering, to bring the Christian witness to bear on the major issues of the day and so to form a part of God's CIA or Christian Intelligence Agency. His call was for Christians to use their knowledge, reason and experience to find new ways to hinder and attack evil and to protect and promote righteousness in society today. Society is not static but changes rapidly, and the Christian needs to be involved in guiding that change.

Foreign policy is an area that is easy to disregard since it involves evaluating one's own nation. Christians are quick to point out to themselves and other Christians the evil in their society but are equally quick to defend that society when it is compared to another nation. That double standard is understandable, but it is neither honest nor wise. The foreign policy of a nation should not be a "sacred cow"; it is simply another area of public policy that can be either good or bad and that can be changed for better or worse. Therefore, Christians should confront the issues and nature of foreign policy.

Christian institutions like churches and colleges, by whatever means they see most appropriate, should address the issues of foreign policy from a Christian perspective. Just as the problems of drug abuse, family life, business ethics, and personal goals and ambitions are made the topics of discussion, so should foreign policy. These institutions should dispense with evasions and platitudes and help their audiences become familiar with the issues and choices, the dangers and implications, the links and the limits of Christianity and foreign policy.

This does not mean that churches or other Christian organizations should take public stands on these issues. This book has tried to make clear the absence of any true and absolute posture for Christians. Foreign policy, like other public policy is subject to varying perspectives and interpretations by different people. There is no Christian Foreign Policy and there is no Christian view of foreign policy. But there is a role for the churches. That role should be to help their members understand world affairs. Current events should not displace the Word of God as the subjects and substance of sermons, but somewhere in the churches the people of God need to deal with issues of foreign policy without tirades and divisions, and without platitudes and panaceas. The attention of pastors, college professors, Sunday school teachers and others to this area of life will contribute to furthering and increasing Christianity as a leaven in American society.

There are positive roles for the individual Christian as well. Just as the American Central Intelligence Agency not only provides information but undertakes actions for change, so the individual should not only keep informed but also act on his beliefs. One simple way is for Christians to write to a senator or congressman.

Communicating with national leaders has to be done in a particular way to be effective. If the letter is just a general statement of support or opposition to an issue, it will be read and tabulated by an assistant in the effort to gauge general public opinion. But if the letter is carefully designed to focus on a particular issue and presents clearly the reasons for support or opposition to a particular policy, then it may well be read and digested by the congressman.

It is also important to write to the senator or congressman, and not to the State Department or Office of the President. Those organizations are prone to pay attention only to those letters that support their policy. If they do recognize letters of opposition, it is only to repackage public statements on policy, not to rethink the policy itself. The reason these organizations take such attitudes is that they are composed of appointed people already committed to their own policies. They are interested in the views of the general public only in terms of support, not in terms of the substance of policy. Their re-evaluation of the substance only comes when they are confronted with other leaders who have some political power over them—a senator or congressman.[3]

Therefore, if you want to really have an impact on foreign policy leaders, you should direct your efforts through the Congress. Letters to Christian congressmen supporting their efforts on particular policies will increase their influence with their colleagues. Letters to your own congressman can influence his opinion. When you write, spell out precise reasons for your position. That will force him to consider those points when he writes a response back to you.

A second activity for Christians is involvement in groups organized to study issues and make presentations to Congress and the bureaucracy. All sorts of such groups exist from which you could choose, depending on your policy preferences. There are groups that are clearly Christian in emphasis and work to present a moral perspective to the government. There are also many nonreligious groups that exist to study foreign policy, or to lobby for particular policies like disarmament, family planning, support of Israel, human rights and famine relief. Or their purpose might be to simply provide information and analysis for the public. If there is an area of foreign policy that interests you, then involvement in one of these kinds of organizations may be a rewarding experience.

A third role is financial. There are always causes that need money and that is true in the field of foreign policy also. A Christian might find the views of a particular candidate or organization similar to his and want to help finance a political campaign for that candidate or finance the activities of that organization. Additionally, there are various relief programs to which a Christian might feel led to contribute, such as UNICEF (United Nations Children's Fund), CARE or a religious program like World Vision's Love Loaf. All these programs and many others like them do a part to alleviate the poverty and hunger that now stalks the southern half of the world. If you cannot be a direct agent in their relief, you can be an indirect agent through one of these organizations.

Beyond that, you may even consider that the manner in which you invest your savings to be a part of your moral concern. There is, for example, a mutual fund organization devoted to investment only in corporations that are not involved in any phase of the manufacture of weapons. This organization, the Pax World Fund, was created because some Christians did not want their savings to be reinvested by regular savings and lending institutions into corporations that produce weapons of war.

The Christian SALT Talks

The United States and the Soviet Union are engaged in discussions and negotiations on limiting the further production of nuclear weapons. These negotiations are called the Strategic Arms Limitation Talks, or SALT Talks.

That acronym SALT reminds us of the characterization of Christians as the salt of the earth. And, as such, they should have a distinctive role to play in discussions of foreign policy. We are the salt because we are to bring out the best in people. Just so, in discussions of national actions in world affairs, we need to act as salt.

Discussions of foreign policy questions are usually highly charged with emotion. They usually involve implications of the rightness or wrongness, or justness or unjustness, or leadership or weakness of the nation. Those implications stir us because of their close and emotional identification with their nation. And soon discussions become heated debates.

Similarly, if the nation is heavily involved in operations abroad and there is widespread opposition, as there was during the Vietnam War, the discussions and debates can become polarized, bitter, hostile and even violent. People can become consumed with defending or opposing specific actions and policies, becoming so committed to truth as they see it that any disagreement with them sours friendships, completely destroys communication and balanced reasoning, and leads to distorted and simplified characterization of people. The peace symbol becomes the "footprint of an American chicken" while defenders of U.S. activity become "war criminals" supporting "genocide." Some people are exhorted to love America or leave it while they are countered with the threat to change America or lose it. Thus blinded by passions, both sides approve or even resort themselves to injustices in the name of moral righteousness.

In this emotional climate of passion and self-righteousness Christians should refrain from any actions that would further inflame the climate of opinion. They should work purposefully to calm passionate debate, to disintoxicate those carried away by fanaticisms and to protect the moderate person from being ridiculed or identified with extremists. Because there is no single true and right position, responsible disagreement must be tolerated and protected both among Christians and within the nation. This role of protecting moderation, of dampening the climate of hostility and of re-establishing rational discussion is an important work for those who are the salt of the earth.

Finally, as the salt of the earth, Christians ought to be involved in developing and promoting activities and projects to heal the emotional, psychological and physical wounds of war. For example, there are various kinds of programs designed to aid disabled veterans who need help and support. The veteran is easily forgotten after the heat of battle for no one likes to remember a war. But they cannot forget. They paid with their bodies and dreams. The local city hall or Veterans of Foreign Wars will provide suggestions on what programs are available or what can be done to begin one in your community.

Recapitulation

In this book I have tried to make three pleas. The first has been a plea for rationality. There is no inherent and objective national interest that is clear and certain. Neither is there a Christian Foreign Policy or clear and certain guides in the Scriptures. Dogma, then, is too superficial and so is too dangerous to be appropriate in an ambiguous and uncertain world. Compartmentalization of religion and foreign policy should likewise be rejected for we do have clear ethical responsibilities to our world's immense problems of war and famine. As committed Christians we live in two worlds. We don't want to get caught between them, caught in bureaucratic "games," media sensationalism, partisan self-justification, or religious self-righteousness. We need to remain aware of events and issues. We need to rationally weigh and evaluate policies and actions. We should not sell our responsibility of judgment for a bowl of clichés and slogans.

The second plea, more implicit, has been for a renewed faith in the potential of this American nation. The United States is still a good country even if the comfortable assumption about being a "Christian nation" has been dashed on the rocks of Vietnam and Watergate. With its bounteous resources, America still carries enormous potential to help, to heal and to build. America is not a discredited nation. The late Senator Robert F. Kennedy, in describing the United States to other countries, coined a phrase which remains apt: We are "just friends and brave enemies."

The third plea has been for involvement on two levels. On one level, all Christians should remain aware of issues and events in U.S. foreign policy. This is the only way to prevent being duped, to understand the need for sacrifices when they become necessary and to be effective as the salt of the earth. For their own protection and for the sake of the contributions they can make, Christians have a responsibility to be in the ranks of the Attentive Public.

On another level, some Christians should get involved in the efforts to create a new concept of policy, a world development policy, a policy of help and service toward those nations and peoples caught in the grip of stultifying and deadening famine and poverty. Such a concept could serve as a guide for American foreign policy. It could serve as a great legitimizing principle of peace, as described in chapter one, to strengthen community. And by doing both of these, it could make a united international effort possible that would decisively reduce human suffering until the return of the Lord. Perhaps we cannot eliminate starvation, terror and war. But as Christians we can be in the vanguard of efforts to work to reduce them. And as Christian citizens of America, in a world of need and danger, that is truly a task worthy of our calling.

Basic Readings
Elbrecht, Paul G. *The Christian Encounters Politics and Government.* St. Louis and London: Concordia. 1965.

Linder, Robert D. & Richard V. Pierard. *Politics: A Case for Christian Action.* Downers Grove, Illinois: InterVarsity Press. 1973.

Pippert, Wesley. *Memo for 1976.* Downers Grove, Illinois: InterVarsity Press. 1974.

Saloma, John S. III & Frederick H. Sontag. *Parties: The Real Opportunity for Effective Citizen Politics*. New York: Alfred A. Knopf. 1972.

NOTES

Chapter One
[1]Richard M. Nixon, "Address by President Nixon at the 124th commencement ceremony, U.S. Naval Academy, June 5, 1974," U.S. Department of State *News Release*, p. 4.
[2]This statement was made by Harvard University nutritionist Jean Mayer and is quoted in *Newsweek*, November 11, 1974, p. 63.

Chapter Two
[1]Niccolo Machiavelli, *The Prince* (New York: A Mentor Book, 1952), pp. 81, 94.
[2]Albert Speer, *Inside the Third Reich* (New York: Macmillan and Co., 1970), p. 82.
[3]See Henry A. Kissinger, *The Necessity for Choice* (New York: Doubleday & Co., 1962), pp. 352-370, and Henry A. Kissinger, "Domestic Structure and Foreign Policy," *Daedalus*, Spring 1966. For a slightly different interpretation, one that sees the capitalistic background and values of officials as decisive in policy-making, see Richard Barnet, *The Roots of War* (Baltimore: Penguin Books, 1971).

Chapter Three
[1]William Shakespeare, *Troilus and Cressida* I, iii.
[2]James M. Hutchens, *Beyond Combat* (Chicago: Moody Press, 1968), p. 25.
[3]Albert Camus, *Resistance, Rebellion, and Death* (New York: The Modern Library, 1960), p. 10.
[4]Boris Pasternak, *Doctor Zhivago* (New York: Signet Books, 1958), pp. 418-19.
[5]John Coleman Bennett, *Foreign Policy in Christian Perspective* (New York: Charles Scribner's Sons, 1966), pp. 45-46.
[6]Winston S. Churchill, quoted in Arthur M. Schlesinger, Jr., *The Bitter Heritage* (Greenwich, Conn.: A Fawcett Crest Book, 1966).
[7]R. Paul Ramsey, "Counting the Costs," in *The Vietnam War: Christian Perspectives*, ed. Michael P. Hamilton (Grand Rapids, Mich.: William B. Eerdmans, 1967), p. 44.
[8]Carl Sandburg, "The Incomparable Abraham Lincoln," in *The Living Words of Abraham Lincoln*, ed. Edward Lewis and Jack Belck (Hallmark Cards, 1967), p. 6.

Chapter Four
[1]Admiral King, quoted in W. W. Rostow, *The United States in the World Arena* (New York: Simon and Schuster, 1960), p. 175.
[2]"Editorial: Engineers and War," *Space/Aeronautics* (November 1967), p. 59.
[3]Maxwell D. Taylor, *Swords and Plowshares* (New York: W. W. Norton, 1972), p. 285.
[4]Robert F. Kennedy, "The 13 Days of Crisis," *The Washington Post*, 3 Nov. 1968, p. B3.
[5]Ibid., 5 Nov. 1968, p. A12.
[6]Herman Kahn, *On Escalation* (New York: Frederick A. Praeger, 1965).
[7]"Notes on McNamara Memorandum for Johnson after Vietnam Visit," Document #107, *The Pentagon Papers* (New York: Bantam Books, 1971), p. 489.

Chapter Five

[1]"Testimony of the Honorable William J. Crockett," *Administration of National Security*, U.S. Senate, Committee on Government Operations (Washington, D.C.: Government Printing Office, 1965), p. 289.

[2]Arthur M. Schlesinger, *A Thousand Days* (Boston: Houghton Mifflin, 1965), p. 406.

[3]"Memorandum of the Honorable Edmund A. Gullion," *Administration of National Security*, p. 482.

[4]Henry A. Kissinger, Speech before Pacem in Terris Conference, Press Release, Bureau of Public Affairs, U.S. Department of State.

[5]A large number of books on the CIA are now appearing. Two of the better ones are Patrick J. McGarvey, *CIA: The Myth and the Madness* (Baltimore: Penguin, 1972) and Victor Marchetti and John D. Marks, *The CIA and the Cult of Intelligence* (New York: Alfred A. Knopf, 1974).

[6]The findings of the Commission were reported in the press. One such report is "The Cloak Comes Off," *Newsweek*, 23 June 1975, pp. 16-19.

Chapter Seven

[1]Gabriel A. Almond, *The American People and Foreign Policy* (New York: Harcourt, Brace and World, 1950).

[2]Ernest W. Lefever, *TV and National Defense* (Boston, Va: Institute for American Strategy Press, 1974).

[3]Bernard C. Cohen, *The Public's Impact on Foreign Policy* (Boston: Little, Brown and Company, 1973), pp. 201-205.

INDEX